You *Can* Pray

You *Can* Pray

By Dana Shrader

MOUNTZ
MEDIA & PUBLISHING

Credits:
Front cover photography—melissakeygallery.com
Back cover photography/logo design—shanelafever.com
Interior design—stonetabletedition@cox.net
Exterior design—jp@collipsis.com

ISBN 978-0-9840673-3-6
You Can Pray
Published by Mountz Media & Publishing
P.O. Box 702398
Tulsa, Oklahoma 74170-2398
918-296-0995
www.mountzmedia.com

DEDICATION

I dedicate this book to
Reverend Judy Talbert
and Victory Tabernacle Ministries.

CONTENTS

FOREWORD

You Can Pray is without a doubt one of the best, most comprehensive studies on Spirit-led New Testament prayer that I have read, and Dana Shrader tackles this subject head on.

Prayer is often thought of as serious, heavy and designed only for those who are "super spiritual." But Dana really opens up the topic, and within the first few pages you realize no matter who you are, no matter what kind of education you have and no matter what your background is—*You Can Pray!*

For those of you who don't know Dana, surprise! She is out of the box, witty, funny, and her humor is disarming. She is also a phenomenal teacher of the Word of God. I would recommend this book for any age—from youth to elders and from denominational to nondenominational—for believers and even for nonbelievers who are searching. This book is a fresh new approach to the topic of prayer.

You won't be disappointed.

Pastor RayGene Wilson
West Coast Believers Church
raygenewilson.com

CHAPTER 1

THE QUESTION **EVERYONE** ASKS

What were you created to do?

Why are you even on this earth?

Have you ever asked yourself these questions? Most people have! In fact, people throughout the world struggle to find the answers. Many people look polished on the outside and appear completely on top of things and supremely satisfied. Yet, everyone has the question deep inside: *What did God create me to do on this earth?*

The truth is, your heart longs to know what you were formed and fashioned to do. This is normal. Ecclesiastes 3:11 says, "He hath put eternity in their hearts...." You were never created just to exist day to day without a plan, a purpose and a pursuit. You won't be happy simply going to the supermarket, to the bank, to work and to bed at 9 p.m. with three squares in between ready to do the same thing all over again and again.

The abilities and gifts you possess long for matching opportunities to impact the world and eternity. Maybe you have battled depression. Maybe you've reached the top of the ladder in your industry or business, yet despite your outward success you still have an inward emptiness or lack of fulfillment. Or, have you found yourself struggling with addictions, poverty and vices? Perhaps people categorize you according to these weaknesses, or maybe you've even defined yourself by these shortcomings and habits.

Nevertheless, somewhere down deep on the inside, you know these tendencies and habits are not the *real* you. Why? Because God has never made a failure. God has never authored anything or anyone who was not glorious for He has made you in the very image of HImself. If you are His child, it is now in your very nature to overcome and succeed. You know His voice, and you are destined for joyous fulfillment.

Are you among many people who are crying out to know God's plan for their lives and feel frustrated and unable to grasp the answer? No wonder—grandma tells you one thing; your mother tells you something else. Your colleagues say, "Hey, you're good at this so you ought to do that." Your spouse has suggestions too. To top it off, society puts an image in your head, and the media paints a picture of what life should be. *You* also have ideas banging around in your head.

So many questions: Who is right? What is right? How can I know for sure? Are these ideas coming from God or my active imagination?

GOOD NEWS

The plan and purpose for your life is as near as your heart and your mouth. It's not lingering out in eternity somewhere. The plan has been formulated and "concreted" into the very foundations of the universe. The plan exists, and it is lodged on the inside of your heart, *begging* to be revealed.

You just need a can opener, as it were. You need something to pop the cork and illuminate your mind to what your heart already knows. How can you "download" for today that ancient scroll called the Bible written about you before time began?

Allow me to introduce to you the handy-dandy, all-purpose-will-of-God-finder, the Ephesians Prayer. Attach this prayer wherever you want to find the will of God. Pray it over a nation to extract the will of God for reaping that nation. Pray it for a sick person who just cannot seem to see himself or herself healed with regard to the scriptures. Watch people's spiritual eyes open and their bodies heal up. Woo hoo! **Attach it to yourself and watch the plans, purposes and pursuits of God rise up on the inside of you and give passion, vision, illumination and revelation of who you really are and what you're called to do.** It's so easy! It's just a prayer away!

People spend so much time banging around in their minds or in their soulish realms trying to *figure out* what God wants them to do. But that won't work because God is not a mind; He is a Spirit. You cannot *figure out* what God wants you to do. *You are a mystery waiting to be revealed, and you must unravel that mystery by revelation and by faith.* Where will you get faith? Faith comes by hearing the Word of God. There is a prayer in the book of Ephesians that will guide you and tell you what to pray. And when you get scriptural, things start happening. When you pray God's Word or the Bible, you *have grounds to hear from God. And when you pray scripturally, God has grounds to hear from you.*

The Bible says we are not to know ourselves after the flesh, but after the spirit. It says we should not know men or women after the flesh, not even Jesus Christ. What does that mean? It means we are to know ourselves and others by faith and revelation. In other words, we are to know each other and God spirit-to-spirit or heart-to-heart.

Here's the deal. If you will pray the prayer found in Ephesians 1:17-23 over and over, you won't have to **figure out who you are supposed to be and what you are called to be.** If you will sow this prayer, you will *reap yourself* or *receive a revelation of yourself.* You will have a revelation of who you are and what you are called to do. Then, your faith will kick in because whatever God has called you to do, you cannot do by your own effort or abilities. You will have to do it by faith, and that way God will get all the glory.

God will be glorified as you discover who He has called you to be and what He has called you to do. Get on the path to discovering who you are. Find out what you are. The Bible calls the born-again believer a new creature, so start praying the Ephesians prayer over yourself and find out what this new creature is like. Let that new creature out for all of us to see. That glorious new creature—the divine you—has been locked up too long.

CHAPTER 2

QUICK ACCESS TO THE WISDOM NEEDED TO **BLOW YOUR MIND** OR MAKE YOU REALLY, REALLY SUCCESSFUL IN LIFE

That's right. The Ephesians prayer is super quick access to the wisdom and revelation of God that's needed to blow your mind or just make you really, really successful in life.

Now you might think the way to pray about the plans and purposes of God for your life would be to go to God in prayer and ask Him what He wants **you** to do. In our own way of doing things, you or I might approach the Father God and say, "Father, I ask You for wisdom and revelation of **me.** I ask for wisdom and revelation and knowledge of **me** and **my calling.**"

However, God has a different way of doing things. In the wisdom of God, He starts off telling His children they are new creations because He knows that every born-again child of God must understand that before he or she can understand *anything at all*.

If you've accepted Jesus Christ as your Savior, something and someone totally new was born—or actually, born again. You were born anew with the life of God injected into your heart. Yes, you probably still order the same kind of pizza, and your favorite color may still be blue. But your spirit or heart—the seat of who you are and why you do what you do—has completely changed.

Your purpose, motives, intents and perceptions of life have been altered. With regard to your heart, it's as though you no longer live, but now Christ lives His life through you. The purpose of your life—and thus, the fruit of your life—now is seemingly hidden with Christ in God. In fact, you are so hidden that evil tendencies, depression and sickness have trouble finding you and attaching to you now because you are in Christ.

You are so *one* with Jesus after you're born again that the Epistles don't even identify you as *you* anymore. New Testament scriptures describe the born-again saint as being *in Him*, using the phrase *in Him* and similar expressions, approximately 140 times throughout the Epistles. So many of the promises of God to the born-again believer refer directly or indirectly to us being *in Him*.

And that's why first and foremost, in order to access these blessings, the believer must satisfy the condition by acknowledging, "Yes, I am now a new creation. Old things have passed away, and now I am clean. I've been made righteous by the blood of the Lamb of God, and I am no longer my own. I am bought with a price. I am literally *in Him*. (Friend, if you're not *in Him*—not born again—you can choose to be right now. Turn to chapter 17 to pray a quick prayer that will change your life forever!)

These *in Him* realities are such revelatory and powerful truths. How can we truly begin to comprehend and even unravel such wondrous things? Thank God, He already thought of that. He has left us a mighty doorway to His wisdom, and *this doorway is but a prayer away*. It is a prayer penned by the apostle Paul found in every King James Bible. It's in every Gideon's Bible in every hotel room. This prayer is not something new fangled and gimmicky—it was authored by a foundational apostle as he was moved on by the Holy Spirit. Of course men of old moved by the Holy Spirit "spoke," but they also "wrote" as the Lord made their tongues as the pen of a ready writer. And so we introduce the powerful Ephesians prayer.

THE MIGHTY EPHESIANS PRAYER

Turn in your Bible to the book or section titled Ephesians, which is found in the New Testament or second half of the Bible. To help you out, let me explain that The Bible is divided into two testaments—the old and the new. It's also divided up into various books and chapters. The books were not originally written this way, but were actually "letters" written from different ministers to different churches. Thus the "book of Ephesians" is a letter from the apostle Paul to the church or group of saints that made up the church in the ancient Greek city of Ephesus.

Now think about this. If this letter was worthy of instruction and blessing to the first saints—then it's still a worthy document of encouragement, instruction and aid to the saints of God today. That's you and me. Hallelujah! *That's why this prayer found in Ephesians 1:17-23 is so powerful—it shows us a key to finding the will of God for our lives.*

Don't approach the Father asking what He wants *you* to do with *your* life. Approach the Father via this mighty Ephesians prayer. Ask Him what this prayer tells you to ask Him. Pray this prayer to the Father and mean it. Then watch His plans and purposes unfold before your spiritual eyes.

Here we go. Turn to Ephesians 1, and let's look at the first few phrases of this prayer in verses 16-18. We can see a confirming consistency.

Ephesians 1:15-18

"Therefore I also, after I heard of your faith in the Lord Jesus and your love for all the saints, do not cease to give thanks for you, making mention of you in my prayers: that the God of our Lord Jesus Christ, the Father of glory, may give to you the *spirit of wisdom and revelation in the knowledge of Him,* the eyes of your understanding being enlightened; that you may know what is the hope of His calling, what are the riches of the glory of **His** inheritance in the saints...."

As we can see here, the language is different from what we would expect. This prayer tells us to ask for wisdom and revelation in the knowledge of **Him**. The verse goes on to reiterate: We want to know the hope of **His** calling in the earth. And if that isn't enough, we are also told to ask "what are the riches of the glory of **His** inheritance!"

Wow! I actually do not even run in to **myself** until I see the end of verse 18, the phrase *"in the saints."* Gee, I don't see **me** until I have prayed first for the wisdom, revelation and knowledge of **Him**. I don't find my calling until I have petitioned to know the hope of **His** calling. I don't find *myself*. I don't see *myself*. I don't know *myself;* I don't find *me, my* calling, *my* enlightenment, *my* understanding or *my* inheritance until I know **Him, His calling** and **His inheritance**.

*The truth is, dear one, as you begin to unravel the mystery of who Jesus is—His calling in the earth and the inheritance He left you—you will come to know who **YOU** are.* As you begin to see His calling, you will unravel your calling. As the Holy Spirit reveals to you the glorious inheritance Jesus left you, you will come to recognize that the glorious inheritance is actually *in you!* You will *never* have to strive and struggle with the will of God again.

If you will simply pray this prayer on a daily basis and combine it with the study of God's Word, you will *simply and suddenly* **know** what you are called to do. You will "run in to" yourself as it were. As you sow this prayer, you will reap direction. As you sow in to the hope of His calling, you will reap your own calling. Within this format, you are seeking first His kingdom and His ways of doing things, so shall all these things—direction and blessings—be added to you.

A RECIPE FOR DIRECTION

I used to be blonde, and I do not cook. However, if I wanted to make a cake or something, I would lay prostrate before the Lord and fast and pray. Ice cubes are really my specialty. If I should venture into the mission field of cooking, I am well prepared; I get a recipe. For me, if there's no recipe, there's no cooking. If there is *no pretty picture on the front of the recipe* card—no vision, no promise of a hopeful end—then "me no cooky." However, if there are clear directions, strict measurements, micro detailing akin to the launch sequence of a NASA Apollo rocket, then and only then, will I endeavor to cook. But keep in mind that I don't go for "a pinch or a dab" or "fold in to" or "shake gently" or any of that stuff. What's with that, anyway? One person's dab may be another persons pinch—especially with the knowledge that a pinch is based on thumb and forefinger sizes that vary greatly. Why do I have to know quantum physics just to make pigs in a blanket?

Once I made a Thanksgiving turkey—though I called the Butterball hotline like 20 times. (Yes, there is a Butterball hotline.) (I trust the operator has not since moved to Cambodia to become a pig farmer.) I burned that turkey so badly no one would eat it. The special sauce I made to "accompany" the fowl was indeed just that—foul. It smelled something like the elephant cage at the zoo. My grandmother, an outspoken and feisty gem, spoke up amidst everyone's horror and asked, "What is that?"

"It's a turkey, Grandma," I told her.

"Well, dear Lord, I would never have known it!" she said. "You've burned it so badly I thought it was a Cornish game hen."

No one present ate even one bite (including me). However, many people had their picture taken with the charred remains.

Anyway, I said all that to say: I love recipes that are as simple as *1 plus 2 equals 3*. I love recipes that promise if you do what the first part says, you'll get the picture on the front of the recipe card. Here's the good news: **The Ephesians prayer is the same way.** Ask for wisdom, revelation and knowledge of Him, ask to know the hope of **His** calling, ask to have an understanding of **His** glorious inheritance, and what you will get is **you—the saint. You** are the final product. **You** are the finished product. **You** are the picture. **You** are what Jesus looks like on the earth today. **You** are fulfilling the plans of the Lord and walking in healing, prosperity and blessings—and that's the picture on the front of God's recipe card.

There's no need for so many Christians to strive in prayer. They're pleading and begging, asking God what they're called to do. They're looking at the road ahead of them trying to figure out which way is right. But when you are praying the Ephesians prayer, you are asking for wisdom and revelation in the knowledge of **Him—and He is the doorway to you and what you are called to do!**

In other words, when we pray the Ephesians prayer we are asking for a revelation of Jesus and wisdom concerning **His** plans on the earth. Of course, we don't know in our natural minds what the wisdom, plan and purpose of Jesus are on the earth. Therefore, when we ask the Father for wisdom and revelation of the Lord's plans, we are stepping out in faith. We are letting loose of our way of thinking and letting loose of our ways of doing things. By faith, then, we are lifted up and out of the confines and impossibilities of the mental arena.

Think about it. This Ephesians prayer is an act of faith. By faith, you launch up and out of yourself because you ask in accordance with the Word of God and release faith for your heart to receive wisdom and revelation of the plans and purposes of God. This biblical prayer spawns faith in your heart!

So don't strive with what to ask, instead submit to the Word. Let 'er go! Dare to lay your plans and your ideas over and upon Him. Go ahead—let yourself seek first His kingdom and His ways. *Then*, all these things you are seeking—your children serving God, financial needs met, loved ones saved and healing in your body—will **overtake you**. The plans and purposes of God will overtake you *because* you are seeking first His kingdom and His ways of doing things.

This prayer will lift you up and out of *yourself*. This prayer will lift you up and out of fleshly reasoning, man's ideas, stinking thinking and every pathway of defeat. Many people testify about the wondrous things the Lord has done for them. Jesus has freed people from drugs, adultery, crime, fear, doubt, oppression, gambling and the list goes on and on. But one of the greatest things Jesus will deliver you from is **yourself!** He will free you from selfishness and that lowly plan only your little brain could come up with. He will free you from living life only for you!

My friend, you were never meant to be the god of your life and the center of your universe. Talk about a black hole! No, you were built to be like Jesus—to give your life and lose your life as it were— so that you may find your life. God has big plans for you! He intends for you to become an absolute blessing to your loved ones, your friends, your family—even the world.

As you pray this prayer, the third person of the Trinity, the Holy Spirit, is freed and authorized to lift you up into the "jet stream" of the plans and purposes of the Lord Jesus for the earth. He will lift you into vistas of revelations of His Word. He will show you nations and peoples. He will impart strategies of reaching out to others. He will even give you a love for others that you never deemed possible. He will ignite the message of the Bible to you. Saints of old now dead will seem as though alive again as they speak through the pages of God's Word showing you how signs, wonders and miracles are still very possible on the earth today.

You will recognize the overall plan of the Lord, and then you will see how *you* fit into that plan. *Your calling will become so evident.* The plan for your life will even seem as if it's simply a byproduct of the overall plan for the earth. There is no doubting; it makes perfect revelational sense.

You see, as you pray the Ephesians prayer you will recognize God's plans for the earth worldwide, even unto the ends of the age. And as you can recognize His plans in this *light*, then you are *walking in His light*. The plans fathered in prayer will never make you a "Lone Ranger." In fact, in this light, you will walk into even more light that will further unify you with the body of Christ. Thus, these "revealed plans" will ever proliferate and regenerate glorious fellowship with the saints of God; you will never be alone again. You will not be alone as an individual, and you will not be alone or apart from divine encouragement, empowerment or the supernatural confirmation only your dear brothers and sisters can provide through the Holy Spirit.

So we see a wondrous outcome—or payoff—in the 18th verse as a result of praying the 17th verse. The Bible promises you that your *very eyes shall become enlightened.* As you begin to walk in revelation and knowledge of God's Word, *your* eyes will begin to be enlightened. You will come to know His voice. In fact, you will come to know so much more than just the words and absolute directions—the black and white—of it all. You will come to know *the tone, the texture, the feel, the sense,* **the Spirit,** *of His callings, leadings and promptings toward you.*

Just as a child knows his or her mother's voice, just as the dog knows his master's voice, just as a sheep knows the shepherd's voice, you will just begin to follow your Leader. You will follow! You *will follow on to know Him.* The Bible promises that **once you hear you will just follow. Truly, the power of the obedience is within the very revelation of hearing.**

Jesus declares that His sheep hear His voice, and His sheep follow Him. Period. That's what He declares. Therefore, dear one, you are His sheep, you do know Him, and because of that, you are following Him. You just are! You just do! You just will! The Word says so!

In John 10:27, the Lord Jesus boldly declares, "My sheep hear my voice, I know them, *(and well)*, **they follow Me!**" Wow! It is just that simple. You simply concentrate on the hearing, and He will work in you both to will and then to do all of His good pleasure (Philippians 2:13). Yes, there is a glorious inheritance in the saints collectively. But, this verse is also saying there is an inheritance of the very glory of God on the inside of each born-again believer—*individually.*

The final sentence in verse 18 gives us a promised blessing for asking the previous sentences. We have asked for wisdom, revelation and an increase in the knowledge of Him so we have fulfilled the condition.

Therefore, these verses crescendo into the promise that we will come to know the *glorious inheritance* on the inside of each of us—that is each and every saint.

Amazing, isn't it? There is an inheritance of the Lord Jesus on the inside of every born-again believer. If you're born again—whether you feel it or not or know it or not—there is an inheritance in **you**. (If you're not born again, turn to Chapter 17 to pray a simple prayer that will take care of that situation!)

Let me explain more about your inheritance. Jesus, the Son of God, died and rose again and left you an inheritance so the legacy of what you are called to do is on the inside of you. The stability of a joyous mind devoid of depression is on the inside of you. A revelation of how healed you already are is on the inside of you. A breakthrough with that family member is on the inside of you.

It's in the last will and testament—if you will—on the inside of *you!* There is a new creation on the inside of you—the real you recreated in Christ Jesus for good works that He predestined you to walk in. It is the glorious inheritance Jesus paid with His life to deposit in each and every saint. The glory of God is your inheritance too. It is as near as your heart and your mouth as you pray this prayer.

The great and mighty Ephesians prayer will draw out and make manifest the Greater One who is living and abiding in you. It's easy—so unfurl that *will!* Your Lawyer will be on hand to help. The Holy Spirit has another name in scripture—the Advocate. So your Lawyer—the Holy Spirit—will guide you in reading your will and announcing your inheritance. Hallelujah—it's but a prayer away. It is but an *Ephesians prayer* away!

As you pray the Ephesians prayer, you will be drawn to situations, events, nations and subjects. Certain things will come to mind, and you will become conscious of different individuals. Perhaps a friend's face will come before you. As it does, go ahead and take an exit in prayer toward that impression. Follow it! Yield to that prompting, to that enlightenment, to that slight nudge from your heart. Dare to pray in your understanding for that friend who comes to mind.

The Ephesians prayer has brought you that prompting by the Holy Spirit, so follow that prompt in faith. Again, I dare you. This time I dare you to believe you are being led by the Holy Spirit. As you do you are stepping out in faith. Begin to pray as best you know how, even though at first your words may be wobbly and unsure. Then, all of the sudden, wisdom and revelation of that friend and his or her situation will begin to well up in you. (Remember, you've been asking for the "spirit of wisdom and revelation," and it now looks like you're beginning to hear from heaven. It looks like your prayers for revelation, wisdom and knowledge are beginning to be answered. The mind of Christ is being manifested and demonstrated in your presence!) From your belly—your innermost being—a knowing of what to pray for and a sudden burst and confirmation of scripture comes forth.

You know things—not by information in your mind—but by revelation from your heart. It's as though things are suddenly revealed to you. My, but what an experience this is! It is almost as though someone greater than you is praying through you and someone greater is—the Greater One Himself. The Bible says, "He who is in **you** is greater than He who is in the world"

(1 John 4:4). And because you stepped out in faith and upon the authority of the scriptures, **someone** has come alongside to **help you** to pray. "...Likewise the **Spirit** also **helpeth our** infirmities: for we know not what we should pray for as we ought: but the Spirit itself maketh intercession..." (Romans 8:26).

As you pray, you sense the compassion of God for that friend. You sense the quickening, the approval and the confirmation of the Spirit in your belly. You rejoice in the overwhelming sense of victory God has for that friend in that situation.

Hmmm, you have just prayed for your friend, and yet through this divine exercise **you** began to learn the *leading* of the Spirit. *You* experienced the *compassion* of the Spirit. **You** came to know the *witness* of the Spirit, and **you** learned how to experience victory in every circumstance. Because **you** stepped out by faith praying the Ephesians prayer and then responded to the Spirit's promptings, **you** know **Him** better. Thus **His** leadings, **His** compassions, **His** witness in your belly, and **His** *victorious voice* will be stronger to you in your day-to-day dealings and decisions. **You** are being sensitized and trained to follow **Him** into **His** prosperity for your life.

You are following **Him** right out of depression, hopelessness and emptiness into **His** purpose, **His** joy, **His** peace and **His** protection. **You** are learning of **Him** and how to leave the hopeless frustration of dealing with your family. Why **you** are even becoming the disciple of the **Father** from whom all **fatherhood** takes its name. **You** are becoming intimately acquainted with the **One** who came up with the idea of families. Dear friend, **He** knows how to help a family function. **You** are learning **His** ways so **you** will recognize **His**

leading to nations and peoples. **You** will come to know the plan of God for **your** life. As **you** pray the Ephesians prayer, **God** answers you with a manifestation of the spirit of wisdom, revelation and knowledge *so shall you follow that same spirit into your calling, into your answers and into every blessing Jesus has for your life.*

CHAPTER **3**

THE **GREATNESS** OF GOD'S POWER

No one ever seems to doubt that God is all powerful. Really, no one in his or her right mind fails to recognize the exceeding greatness of the power that belongs to the Creator of the universe. But did you know that God has also delegated power to His children?

Let's look further into the great and mighty Ephesians prayer that teaches us about the power of God. We have looked closely at verses 17 and 18, but now let's delve in to verses 19 through 21 that look specifically at the *power* of God.

The power of God in this passage is referred to as *"the exceeding greatness of His power."* Because we have already asked for wisdom and revelation in the previous verses, the "power" of God begins to manifest. In fact, the Ephesians prayer is a perfect portrait of this divine sequence. The power of God manifests on the heels of wisdom, revelation and knowledge. The Holy Spirit, the One who manifests the power of the Godhead, always comes to confirm the Word.

As we put the Word first, wisdom, revelation and knowledge are all extracted from the Word of God. Why? Because the Word is the source of all true wisdom, revelation and knowledge. Thus when the Word is first place, the Holy Spirit of God can and will manifest the exceeding greatness of the power that even raised Jesus from the dead.

As you come to know the power by revelation, you will begin to speak out of your mouth what God has said. Then, as you know and speak, situations will change because God has delegated the power to you. Amazingly enough, if you're born again you already possess more than enough faith because you've been given a measure of the God kind of faith. So as you become convinced of what already belongs to you, you will simply speak and your body, your finances, your situations—*even you*—will change.

Ephesians 1:19-21 instructs us to pray that we may come to **know**...

"...what is the ***exceeding greatness of His power*** toward us who believe, according to the working of His mighty power which He worked in Christ when He raised Him from the dead and seated Him at His right hand in the heavenly places, far above all principality and power and might and dominion, and every name that is named...."

In this prayer, we ask to *know* (by experience the working of, and even effects of) the *exceeding greatness of His power*. This *power* is further defined in this prayer as *the power that raised Jesus from the dead and set Him in His place of authority throughout the universe* (and throughout every situation, event and facet of your person and your life).

Wow! *God is so excited about you experiencing that same power that raised Jesus from the dead that He gave you a prayer to ask for it.* First John 5:14-15 says, "...If we ask anything (make any request) according to His will ... He listens to and hears us ... and ... we have ... the requests made of Him" (AMP).

The reality is, if God Himself has put this prayer in the Bible—a prayer to *know* by revelation and experience the very *power* that raised and seated Jesus—then *God will* **show, display** *and* **communicate** *that power to all who pray this prayer.* The answer is yes and amen.

The power exuded at the resurrection of Jesus Christ is the *absolute greatest display of power that God the Father ever exercised.* In fact, the very act of raising Jesus from the dead is defined as the **"exceeding greatness"** **of His power.**

Psalms 8 tells us that God used His *fingers* to spangle the heavens with the stars. "When I consider Your heavens, **the work of Your fingers**, the moon and the stars, which You have ordained..." (verse 3). Exodus 15:8 says that Father God used a blast of His **nostrils** to split the Red Sea for Moses. Isaiah 52:10 and Isaiah 59:16 speak of the **arm** of God. Isaiah 59:16 tells us *"...His own* **arm** *brought* **salvation** *for Him."* Isaiah 52:10 says, "The Lord has **made bare** His holy **arm...."**

Think about this. When a handyman gets ready to lift something heavy or do some real work, he rolls up his sleeves and bares his forearm. And that's exactly what God did to raise Jesus from the dead. What a moment that was! When God raised Jesus from the dead, He also raised you and me. He raised every Christian past, present or future from the power of death, hell and the grave. So great was this manifestation of power that it raised the Church to glory, victory and the sphere where impossibilities are made possible. At the same time, God also dismantled, broke and crucified the powers of darkness so they would never again dominate the blood-bought saints of the Lord Jesus Christ.

What kind of power are we talking about? Well, let's see what the Ephesians prayer says about this particular manifestation of God's power. This power we are praying to know first of all raised Jesus from the dead. Of course, the Bible tells us about many saints who have been raised from the dead such as Lazarus. Jesus stopped a funeral and raised a young man from the dead. In fact, there are many people beyond Bible days who have returned from the brink of death. There are people who've been raised from the dead on the mission fields of the world.

Yet, the prayer found in the book of Ephesians is very specific. We are not instructed to pray to know the power that has raised different saints from the dead. We are told to ask—and to know by experience—the power that raised **Jesus** from the dead. The Bible defines the power that raised Jesus from the dead as **the exceeding greatness of the power of God.**

Therefore, the resurrection of **Jesus from the dead** was **different than any other resurrection from the dead**. God's power not only made Jesus alive again, but God also exuded enough power to heal Jesus from that which killed Him. Glory to God, Jesus didn't just come up alive, Jesus came up **different.**

In the Gospel chapters after the resurrection, Jesus is not at all the same. He had a **different body**. He told the disciples to handle Him for a spirit "hath not *flesh and bones*" (Luke 24:39). Jesus said nothing of blood because He's not running on blood any more. His blood is now before the mercy seat in heaven. He is not flesh and blood anymore. Jesus has just said He's now made up of **flesh and bone**. So it looks like He's running on pure glory. Glory! The life of God is coursing through His very veins.

Jesus no longer enters rooms through doors anymore. After the resurrection, the language of the Gospels describe Him as "appearing" and "manifesting." Those closest to Him no longer recognize Him at first. Things are very different; His **body is different**. I like to say in plain lingo: His body is **made alive**, **refried** and **glorified!**

People long for the supernatural, and here it is. People watch *X-Files*, *Star Trek*, *Star Wars* and anything else "interplanetary." They wonder, *Hey, how were those crop circles made, anyway? The National Enquirer* has headlined every kind of mutation known to the imagination. Yet when it comes to the Bible, people get all stiff and rigid and boring—which equals *unscriptural*.

Some people think the Bible is boring and that a person has to wear a choir robe to read it. But I've got news: There's nothing boring about the Bible. At times a person could label it *E.T.* because there are scriptural extraterrestrials right in the Gospels. Yeah— Jesus came from a foreign place all right, and He has a different body. Jesus right now has a body that can function in heaven, in space or on the earth. His wild body can walk through walls, fly, disappear and reappear. Mark 16:12 even says Jesus at one point after the resurrection "appeared in another *form*." *What?!* That's wild! That's awesome! You can read this stuff—it's real, and there's no cable bill!

Not only is Jesus like E.T. supernatural, but also you and I are destined to have a body like His someday. Woo hoo! Yes, there is a heaven to gain and a hell to shun with salvation. But, dude, for sure I want to get this wild-freak-o-rama-flying-saucer-like-DNA-altered-wicked-awesome space suit. First Corinthians 15:40 tells us that **we** are so scripturally destined to have this kind of body it even uses the word *extraterrestrial* in the scriptures. Dude—we are like so E.T.! Get this! When you pray the Ephesians prayer, you are like E.T. *phoning home.* Major-surfs-up–hang-10-dude-I-got-starfish-stuck-in-my-wetsuit awesome! (I once preached at a women's meeting in a wetsuit. It was a beach theme. If I come to your church to preach, I will explain. Otherwise, no details!)

Now, do you get it? It's no wonder you love *X-Files!* God has put eternity—and its mind- and body-altering laws—in your heart. (Agent Fox Mulder is so awesome! My favorite *Star Trek* shows are the old ones, especially "The Trouble with Tribbles." Better pray you're not the extra guy in a red shirt getting beamed to the surface—or man, you're a goner!)

E.T. aside for now, the power that raised Jesus from the dead did not stop there. The exceeding greatness of the power you are praying to know—*that* power changed the very composition of the body of Jesus. That power also shot Jesus down into hell. That power enabled Him to take the keys of death, hell and the grave away from the devil.

At the time of the resurrection, the graves of dead saints were opened and many were seen up and walking in Jerusalem. So much power was exuded at the resurrection of Jesus that it not only changed Him, but that power also overflowed His grave and raised up the bodies of those who had died in faith. Think about it. This is a preview of the resurrection!

At a moment, at the twinkling of an eye—a final increment and flash of light—we like our Master will be made alive and glorified. And that same power will jerk the bodies of the dead in Christ from their graves. This gospel portrait of the resurrection is but a **preview** of the redemption of our own mortal bodies. The same Spirit who raised Jesus from the dead will quicken and make alive our mortal bodies. How all of creation is longing for the revealing of the sons of God. It will be a **revealing**; it will be a **revelation** given to the saints. Isn't it interesting that the Ephesians prayer asks specifically for **revelation of the resurrection power. We are to know the power—we are to experience, enjoy and administer the power.**

Still, the power did not stop there. So much power! The scriptures deem it, "the **exceeding greatness**" of God's power. That power then **lifted Him up, above principalities, above powers.** That power also lifts **you** up above any demonic power that tries to influence you and your life. Please understand that the word lift doesn't mean He just floated upward. By definition it means He dismantled and made to no avail the powers of principalities and powers. He took away the authority and power of the spirit that would influence you toward depression, defeat, fear, lack, sickness and death.

Then the power lifted Him up above even **might** and **dominion.** The Bible speaks of the **dominion of**

death. Jesus has delivered those who through fear of death were held in bondage to it their entire lives. How did Jesus set us free from the fear of death? He conquered death. If you have asked Jesus into your heart, then you will live forever with Him. You will go through one of two portals—either the portal of the grave or the exhilarating entrance of the rapture of the Church. Either way, brother and sister, your body will undergo the power of the resurrection, and you will have a body perfectly adapted to express your spirit man, a body that knows no impossibilities or limitations.

Let's look again at the Ephesians prayer. Ephesians 1:20 uses unusual language to describe the present-day authority of the Lord Jesus, the authority He earned, bought and paid for with His own blood. That authority became His through the conquest of the Cross. Ephesians 1:20 says, "...which He worked in Christ when He raised Him from the dead and **seated** Him...." In other words, the power of the resurrection **seated** Jesus or established Him in a seat of authority at the right hand of the Father God.

To really get the point here, let's consider the "seat" of authority for the United States or the literal chair of the president of the United States. Most likely there is a tidy little maid who cleans the Oval Office and dusts on a regular basis. Let's suppose one day she dusts for quite a while and gets a little tired. Suppose she even sits down in the president's chair and plops her feet up on his desk. Who knows— maybe she even decides to take a piece of paper and write a proposal. Let's say the proposal states that all maids should receive paid vacations to Hawaii annually. Now she's sitting in the president's chair writing a proposal, so why is it that her proposal from the Oval Office will have no power? The proposal has no power because the tidy little maid was not **seated** by a national vote. She has no authority granted to her by the American people. She might be sitting in the chair, but she was not **seated** in authority. It takes the power of a national vote to seat a person into authority.

However, the exceeding greatness of the power of God seated Jesus in a place of authority, and the right hand of the throne of God is the center of power of the entire universe. Jesus is seated there to rule and reign, far above all principalities, powers, might and dominion.

Now, guess what? If you're a Christian, you are seated there with Him! He said so!

You also are far above all principalities, powers, might and dominion. You are so far above them that they are under your feet. No matter what it looks like or feels like, you are seated above the powers of the enemy. You are seated with Jesus, and you have already overcome the enemy. It may not look like or feel like you have overcome the enemy, but you have because Jesus overcame the devil 2,000 years ago. The Bible calls **you** an overcomer! All you need is a **revelation** of the exceeding greatness of the power that seated you. You need a revelation, and thank goodness, God gave you the Ephesians prayer to access that revelation. You don't have to figure out blessings in your head. You can just pray the Ephesians prayer and "*revelate*" your blessings from your spirit to your head.

Positionally and doctrinally you are already seated with Jesus if you're born again. But as you pray the

Ephesians prayer, you will be seated with Jesus **experientially.** Go on—experience the power He paid for and experience your place of victory. That power is your legacy and your inheritance. It's already yours! Pray the Ephesians prayer for revelation that you may access the power of that exaltation.

Many Christians have found by simply praying the Ephesians prayer with regard to whatever form of sickness that has attacked their body, they will receive a revelation of how very healed they are. Many Christians are crying out to the Lord regarding the ravaging pain, the ominous diagnosis and the overwhelming physical weakness they feel. We do not deny the existence of these things—such suffering of mankind certainly exists. Yet, my dear friend, sympathy and soft words will not ease your physical war. But *a revelation of the truth of God's Word will drive off the onslaughts that wish to overtake and rule your temple.* If you will but take the mighty Ephesians prayer and insert the word *healing* throughout it, the Holy Spirit will be released to teach you, *to convince you,* declare to you, transmit to you and access for you the very power that raised Jesus from the dead.

The Bible says in Romans 8:11 that the same power that raised Jesus from the dead will even *quicken your mortal body.* If the full measure of this power can transform you to meet Him in the air, just think what a dab of it will do to cancer, AIDS or bronchitis. To know this power that raised Jesus from the dead will *make things alive!*

Romans 8:11

"But if the Spirit of Him who raised Jesus from the dead dwells in you, He Who raised Christ from the dead will also give life to your mortal bodies through His spirit who dwells in *you!*"

Hallelujah! All the power you need is not found in someone else. It's not all bottled up in heaven. No way. All the power you'll ever need is on the inside of *you*.

It's so easy to pray this prayer for healing in your body. You can talk to God like this: "Father, it's awesome that Jesus did all those miracles in the Bible. But Father, up to now the common cold (or whatever) has had me beat! But I am going to apply your Word to this situation and trust in your Word." Then apply the Ephesians prayer with the word *healing* or your situation inserted within its context.

Say, for example, your affliction is "cancer." Then insert that disease into the prayer like this: "Father God, I ask You for the spirit of wisdom and revelation with regard to your healing power and this cancer. Regarding your healing power, I ask for a greater knowledge of You that *my* eyes would be enlightened regarding Your healing power. I ask for a greater knowledge of Your will regarding healing and how very healed I am already of cancer! I ask that I would know the glorious inheritance on the inside of me regarding this cancer. I ask that I would come to know the exceeding greatness of the power that raised Jesus from the dead.

"I ask that I would come to know by revelation and experience that same power that killed what Jesus killed—that same power that pronounced death to the death that would have tried to overcome Jesus. I ask that through revelation I would with my own mouth swallow up death in victory. I cannot do it in my own flesh or with my own determination or will. But I can cry out to you via Your Word—through this mighty Ephesians prayer—and You will by the power of the Holy Spirit, prompt, teach and **convince** me of how healing already belongs to me. You will convince me of how healed I already am. I put all my trust in Your Word and in Your Spirit. You have come to deliver me from the power of doubt, fear and death."

Pray the whole prayer from your guts—meaning it, believing it, working it before the Father. When you pray this scriptural prayer things start to happen. Things always start to happen when you get scriptural! The next time you open your Bible to read, watch how the passages of Jesus healing people begin to jump out at you. Watch how different scriptures begin to break open as never before. Your eyes begin to be enlightened. As you are prompted into encouragement and soothed by a peace that passes your understanding, your body will begin to respond. Symptoms will ease. Joy will spring forth and with it comes the *strength which God gives.* The Lord will take hold of you and begin to lead you, and He will guide you right up and off of the bed of affliction.

Yeah, though you seem to be walking through the valley of the shadow of death, you will have no fear. His rod and His staff, they are *comforting you.* He *is* preparing for you a table in the midst of your physical enemies of disease and sickness (Psalm 23). You will eat well and bountifully. You will taste and see that the Lord is *good* (Psalm 34:8). Jesus goes about *doing good* and healing you of all of your afflictions (Act 10:38). He is your *good* Shepherd. He is leading you into *green pastures*—green, I say! He is leading you to pastures that are *full of life*—pastures that *make you alive.* And there, in the midst of life, He will even make you to lie down and rest—*lie down in a field of life.*

See, even right here, in the midst of writing these paragraphs, the Holy Spirit has spoken up. In the very penmanship of the previous paragraph, He is beginning to convince you of His healing power for you. He is taking scripture after scripture like a pharmacist mixing your prescription and putting together blocks of life, unction and power to convince you of your healed and disease-free state. It is in this transformed state that you are conformed to His glorious body where there is no pain, no sickness, no weakness and no defeat.

God is glorified in this place of faith—a place where your mind, will and emotions have been convinced of victory. He has defeated death, hell and the grave! He is raised up to a place where there is no sickness. He was raised to this place *by the exceeding greatness of the power of God,* and *you* are raised with Him. As you make requests to know the exceeding greatness of His power, you are coming into a revelation, and you will experience the demonstration of that same arm of power that crushed sickness, sin, death, hell and the grave. **Wow! As Christians you and I are seated so very far above.**

Still, the power does not stop there. Ephesians 1:21 goes on to tell us that not only are we seated above principalities, powers, might and dominion, but we are also seated, **"far above every name that is named!"** Jesus' name is above every name that is named. And if you have received Jesus as your Savior, then **you** are *in Him.* More than 140 times you'll read phrases such as *in Him* and similar expressions in the New Testament, and each will be talking about **you.**

You have taken His name—and that name is now also your name. What does that mean? In the simplest of terms it means *if something has a name, then the name of Jesus is above it. Since you have the name of Jesus now, then* **you also are far above everything that has a name.** So if something is bothering you—a sickness, a worry, a financial woe—they are still all names. They are **names** of problems. A name was all that problem needed in order to qualify—now Jesus and you are far above that thing. That makes that problem under your feet.

CHAPTER 4

JESUS HAS **BIG** FEET

"And hath put **all things** under **His feet**...."

Ephesians 1:22, (KJV)

Christians have lots of benefits, and Ephesians 1:22 makes that clear. The scripture goes on to offer us a fuller picture and an excellent illustration of what we have gained in Christ. Verse 22 tells us that Jesus is the name above every name and that God the Father hath put **all things** under the feet of Jesus.

And let's face it—Jesus has big feet!

His feet are so big Psalm 99:5 declares the earth is but the footstool of God. Since you are *in Him*—that means **you** have big feet too. You are in Jesus, and therefore, you have full use of His feet. Interestingly enough, in Genesis 3:15 God the Father said of Adam that the devil would bruise his heel. But in the end, Adam would crush the serpent's head. One way to crush the head of a serpent is to step on it.

When it comes right down to it, Jesus paid a great price for you to have big feet. He allowed a nail to pierce His feet, and the weight of His body and the sins of the world to rest upon that wound so that now the body of Christ might carry the gospel to the world. How lovely are the feet of them who preach good news.

Think about all the things your big feet can walk on. Do you have a sickness? Maybe its name is AIDS? Well, AIDS is under your feet just like every other symptom or disease. Step on that thing. Speak to that thing called sickness. Speak to that thing called AIDS. Don't be like Eve and entertain a snake. Don't let that snake tell you to bear sickness and disease. Step on it! Tell it: "Oh, no you don't AIDS!" Don't let that lie crawl and slither through the home of your heart and affect what you believe. Don't allow creeping and crawling lies to nest in your mind and plague your thoughts.

Start talking truth: "Jesus bore death for me. He laid His life down so that I might live! In Jesus' name you can't kill me!" Squash it like a bug. Drop kick it. Go ahead and dance for joy on the head of that disease because if you are a Christian that disease is under your feet. You are far above the symptoms and the ultimate diagnosis of doom. Crush the serpent's head and enforce the victory Jesus won again and again. You will live and not die and declare the works of the Lord (Psalm 118:17).

You can walk all over a lot more than sickness. How about attitudes and bad behavior? Maybe someone is trying to sue you, or maybe someone is being mean to you. These truths of victory apply to *anyone* or *anything* trying to harm you. If that person has a *name*, then the *effects* of that person are under the name of Jesus. Do not lash out at that person. You are far above the warfare, strife and bickering of the world. You are far above "brown-nosing" and "playing politics" at your job. The person bothering you is not your enemy; the devil is your enemy and *even his name is under your feet!*

You are far above strife, unforgiveness and believing the worst about people. You are seated far above revenge and "elbowing your way past" other people. You are seated so very far *above* those situations— even at the right hand of the Father. You are seated with the "Boss" of all bosses. Believe me; you are in direct contact with the true head of human resources. If you will stay true to your employee handbook of the Bible, you will always have the will of God in your life and things will *always work for your good in the end.*

So, I double-dog dare you to pray for that person who seems to be your enemy. Go ahead! Tap in to your true nature. You have the nature of God on the inside of you. First Corinthians 13 says you have the capacity to love, to take no account of a suffered wrong and to even believe the best of the most "devilish-acting" people. So great is the extent of God's love in your heart that Jesus said you have the ability to forgive someone 70 x 7 times a day for doing wrong to you. Talk about miracles!

The disciples' response to this great task when Jesus taught them on forgiveness was, "Lord, increase our faith!" But, hey, you can do it! You have the love of God in your heart just as they did. As you love and forgive people by faith, feelings will follow. You forgive them by faith, you bless them by faith. You live by faith! You do good to your enemies *by faith.* **Then,** later, after you have acted in faith, feelings of forgiveness will come. Thoughts and detailed tallies of wrongdoings toward you will melt away; you will forget about them as the love of God sets you free. As you get busy doing the will of God, the stain and the sting of those hurtful things are sponged away.

You are so far above those satanically inspired acts and words that you will pray for your enemies. You will pray for them and even do good to them. What did that preacher lady just say? Do **good** to them? Yeah, that's right!

So if someone has hurt you or wronged you, here's what you do. First, take authority and put the devil in his place. You say, "No, you don't devil!" Then set about praying to your heavenly Father saying: "Father God, in the name of Jesus, thank You for granting me favor. You are surrounding me with favor like a shield. No matter what it looks like or feels like, I say I come out smelling like a rose. I believe it by faith, Father. I believe it so much that I'm going to act like all is well and even pray blessings down upon that person who sought to do me harm and say: No evil report against me will prosper. I trust in Your mercies, Father, even if I did do wrong."

Then, buddy, watch the miracles start happening. Send that person a gift or give him or her some money. *You must be kidding?* No, I'm not. You are far above the ways of the world! The peace of Jesus is headed your way, and His peace will be made known to you because you have become a peacemaker in your relationships.

Pray for your enemies and do good to them. You will access the peace of God for yourself. It's peace that surpasses your mind and ability to figure it all out, and it's a peace that surpasses your emotions. Here you are: *praying* for your enemies, *sowing* peace and *reaping* peace. This is the peace of Jesus. His "brand" of peace is so deep and powerful it's like a garrison mounting over your heart and mind, **guarding your heart and keeping it engaged in faith.**

This garrison keeps out—and blocks—bitterness, resentment, evil thoughts, oppression and cares that could lead you astray and out of the plans of God. This peace is the perfect umpire so let it rule and reign in your heart. Let the umpire of peace call "out" or "safe" with regard to thoughts of bitterness or revenge that try to slide into your consciousness and make it home. "Out" to bitterness. Jesus could have been bitter but He said, "Father forgive them." "Out" to revenge.

"Safe" is the haven of trusting in the Lord. "Safe" are your prayers as you stand praying and forgiving by faith those whom you have ought against. Begin to pray: "I forgive them by faith, O Lord. I don't forgive them based on the way I feel, but by faith I call them forgiven."

Let me say that if you're among those who have endured terrible abuse and literal crimes of a physical and an emotional nature, these rules of forgiveness in no way deny or excuse what happened to you. The heinous nature of the order of this world is why Jesus Himself could not stay in heaven, but clothed Himself in flesh and entered earth's atmosphere to intervene. He purposely endured torture and torment for you. The Bible dares to say He literally **became sin** so you and I would **become the literal righteousness of God in Him.**

That means He took upon Himself every horror a

human could experience. Yet, He knew the pathway to true freedom and life everlasting would be to display a "way of escape." That ultimate way of escape—the great key of freedom—was when He uttered from the Cross **out loud** for the whole world to hear, "Father, forgive them, for they know not what they do." He could have prayed silently. But truly even the men who tortured Him heard it. Even the disciples heard it and wrote it in the Bible for you to see. Jesus wanted to make sure **you** heard it, for it is your answer. God is the only One who **can** and **will** reach into the deepest parts of your soul and make it brand new. Just let Him, dear one! By following His path—this path that seems so different and contrary to what you feel—you'll walk in His path of forgiveness by faith.

When you pray in faith this way you are then living far above all principality, power and dominion, and you have escaped the ways of the world. You have overcome the fleshly tendency to "fight back" or "get even." You have escaped the lie of having to "make people pay or make people suffer for what they have done." You have overcome dealing with these situations the way the "worldly mind-sets" would dictate.

Therefore, because you have overcome these fleshly situations by the Word and the Spirit, you are *free from the effects* of these hurtful situations, memories and people. You have overcome them and the truth has set you free indeed. You are truly free! You have identified with the name that is above everything, anyone and anything that has a name. You are absolutely seated far above!

CHAPTER 5

THE REAL **SCI-FI** CHANNEL

---

*S*tar Wars, *Star Trek* and the Sci-Fi channel have nothing on the Bible. The ultimate destination of every Christian is not the finite world of this dirt ball we call earth. Our home, our destiny—the place from which we have come, the place we've not seen with our physical eyes yet know so well in our hearts—that heavenly city is the place to which we are all "hard pressed" to go.

Paul the apostle so aptly states in Philippians 1:23-24, "having a desire to go but it is more needful for you that I stay...." No, these are not the maniacal ravings of a suicidal escapist. They are statements of love and motivation that caused the apostle Paul to pen revelations we still are believing to unravel. These same mind-sets of Paul were also what propelled him to his missionary journeys and empowered him to establish churches nationally and internationally. Eternity beckoned to him. The celestial, glorious and heavenly city was always in his sights, becoming clearer and dearer with each day he would obey in terrestrial pursuits.

You see, Ephesians chapter 1:21-22 tantalizes us with a promise of just how far revelation knowledge will take us. Oh, the realms that this amazing tour guide and pilot known as the Ephesians prayer will take us.

Look again at **Ephesians 1:21-22:**

"...far above all principality and power and might and dominion, and every name that is named, **not only in this age but also in that which is to come.**"

This is my favorite part of the Ephesians prayer. It reminds me of another scripture that says, "He has put eternity in their hearts..." (Ecclesiastes 3:11). The truth is every man, woman and child longs for the supernatural; we long for a presence or a world greater than ourselves. This is one reason I love to preach this prayer to children, youth and the college and career age. Young people are so innocent and excited about everything, and they have not quenched even the possibility of the supernatural.

Ephesians 1:21 goes on to tell us that we are seated far above principalities, powers, might, dominion and every name that is named, " ... *not only in this age but also in that [age or world] which is to come."* Isn't that amazing? Our authority as Christians stretches not only throughout this age, but it also reaches into the age that is to come. That "age to come" is heaven—it is eternity. It is the place where there is no sadness, no sickness, no poverty.

When we pray this prayer found in Ephesians, we come to know a revelation of our Savior and a taste of the powers of heaven. This prayer causes us to find our place to reach the harvest and helps us to bring in the harvest of souls. All the while, this prayer *prepares* us to meet the Lord. **Lord, prepare us for that which you have prepared for us.**

Here's the bottom line: Jesus is coming very soon. And this prayer lines up the saints for that event. This prayer promises a revelation of Jesus. It promises we will find our place of service to reach the lost, and it promises to let us taste and experience the place where we are headed. The age to come—the portal to the next place—is as near as you finding your place in the body of Christ. It is as accessible as you asking for revelation and learning to flow with and yield to the exceeding greatness of His power.

Dear reader, did you know that the New Testament scriptures promise that Jesus will again return and take His Church to heaven with Him? He will not come all the way down, but in fact, His Church—His very bride—**will go up to meet Him**. (1 Thessalonians 4:17). Wow! What does all that mean? I don't exactly know, and I don't have to know. I just have to believe and then I will know! Awesome.

Since the scriptures promise that we the Church will go out to meet our beloved groom, (Matthew 25:5-8) "the Lord Jesus," this means that the Church will *have a part* in the going out to meet Him. The Church will be so proficient in moving in the things of God that we will even meet him halfway—in a meeting in the air—a spiritual place. Dude, that is awesome!

So this prayer can become our flight simulator. We get to work with the exceeding greatness of the power that *raised Him*. We get to "practice" with that power on a daily basis. We can practice overcoming sickness in our bodies. We can also practice overcoming doubt, fear, unbelief, gossip, backbiting, jealousy and hatred. We practice lifting up and out of debt and financial poverty. We practice with the same power that raised Jesus and overcomes on a daily basis until that day when we will **come over** to Him—*raised by that same power with which He arose.*

Whoa—we come over to Him raised by that same power with which He arose. *Woo hoo!*

Again, I very soberly, reverently and respectfully say, dude, that is so awesome wondrous! It blows my mind and completely rewires my brain. It renews the spirit of my mind! It's severely cool!

Dude, it's going to be like sooo easy to go in the rapture. (The *rapture* is a word that Christians often use to describe the return of the Lord. This term *rapture* is not formally in the Bible, however, it is a term Christians coined regarding the specific event of the Second Coming of the Lord that *is* **like-so-most-definitely** in the Bible.) (If you're not absolutely positive you're born again and ready to take flight when Jesus returns, turn to Chapter 17 and pray a quick and life-changing prayer right this minute!)

Now think about this. If the Bible tells us to pray for a revelation that will access the exceeding greatness of God's power, that *is* the power that glorified the body of Jesus and seated Him at the right hand of the Father. *Then,* when we pray that prayer, we are setting ourselves on the same pathway that Jesus took. Jesus at present is seated at the right hand of the Father in a glorified body, ruling and reigning in eternity. If we pray this prayer asking to know the exceeding greatness of the power that raised Jesus from the dead and seated Him in a glorified body at the right hand of the Father, we will ultimately experience the same power. We will be freed from our earthly bodies bound for death. Our bodies will be changed, glorified, made eternal, and we also shall sit at the right hand of Father God for all eternity.

The Ephesians prayer tells us to ask for a revelation and a demonstration of this power. The Ephesians prayer tells us to pray to know this same pathway of victory. Therefore, if the Word of God tells us to ask for this and every promise of God is yes and amen, then we have and will have those things we ask of Him. We shall know this same power and experience and ultimately the same place of glory, authority and fellowship that Jesus knows. Hallelujah! Totally Awesome! Severe kewlness! Right on! This is so exciting that a series of smiley icons depicting radical joy should have been placed here. I'm so fired up that I think I just got a sunburn. Does anybody have some kind of moisturizing lotion? Wooo Hooo!

Ultimately, this prayer sets us on a course for our bodies to be altered, lifted up and brought near to our Lord to rule and reign throughout eternity. He has already told us in Ephesians 5 we are bone of His bone and flesh of His flesh.

The rapture of the Church is not something you must strive for or fear. If you simply pray this prayer found in Ephesians, you will experience revelation as never before. In fact, you will follow in the footsteps of Jesus. Remember where that same power first took Jesus? It took Him right straight to hell. And when you pray this prayer, God the Father will fire you into the place of the harvest where you also will plunder hell. As you pray the Ephesians prayer, the first thing that will happen is the revelation of the plan, purpose and pursuit of the will of God will come forth. You will begin to see your place in the overall harvest field of the world. Like Jesus, you will set the captives free.

Then one day—in an instant, in the twinkling of an eye, in a glimmer of light, in one more increment of revelation, your eyes being enlightened—you will be changed. The revelation will evolve into and elicit the exceeding greatness of His power. In the midst of your place of service in the harvest field, you shall be lifted up, translated. The Bible says those who are alive and remain shall simply step up and over principalities, powers, might and dominion. So you will find yourself in a body that is glorious and new. Isn't that awesome! You are the ultimate alien! You are the personification of the Sci-Fi Channel—Wooo hooo! No one is cooler than our Savior!

This revelation and empowerment is for everyone from children to the elderly, and it's so easy—as easy as getting saved. To get saved or born again a person simply hears a revelation, believes and then is translated from darkness to light. (If you're not born again, see for yourself what it's all about by turning to Chapter 17! You could consider the Ephesians prayer like an "update" for those who have downloaded the "software" of asking Jesus into their heart. You can use the program or the Ephesians prayer limitedly, but to really get the full benefits you have to download your software and get an account with the Lord Jesus Christ. You can just turn to Chapter 17, pray that quick prayer, and then come right back here and continue reading. Dude—it's awesome! Once your account is created, you'll get more updates. You also get the ultimate email service to and from the Lord Himself. There are no viruses and no passwords to remember. Forget the world wide web—this is the ultimate guide to the galaxy! I think I hear the *Star Trek* theme, and Optimus Prime just turned my Honda into a cage fighter.)

Even better, it *will be just that easy to go be with the*

Lord someday. Those who have harvested God's will for their lives via the Word and then harvested knowledge of their place in the harvest field have already experienced the power of the resurrection to separate, send and place. And that same power shall also separate, send and seat them with Jesus upon His soon and evident return. Hallelujah!

So easy

just a revelation that causes sight

and thus a power that culminates in flight,

the draft of which,

raises the saints who have gone before,

the Christians,

who will pray in the present,

this prayer,

those who are alive and remain,

will become a door.

The past and future come together in the "I AM,"

and so shall we ever be with the Lord,

together,

at last.

Amen.

CHAPTER 6

YOUR **PLACE** IN THE BODY OF CHRIST

"...the church, Which is his body, the fulness of him...."

Ephesians 1:22-23 (KJV)

The final verses of this mighty Ephesians prayer are the very answer to the prayer you've been praying. Think of these final verses as the conclusion or the result of praying all the previous parts of this prayer. After all, *the ultimate answer for the person praying the mighty Ephesians prayer is the **manifestation of the will of God for that person**. That means a natural— actually, a very supernatural—byproduct of praying the Ephesians prayer is that *you* will find your place in the body of Christ. You will find your destiny.

When we pray the Ephesians prayer, we are asking for the wisdom of God; we are asking for the overall mind-set of God. By faith, we will be tapping into the wisdom and revelation of God to reap the world. It is a high place. As we pray the Ephesians prayer, we will be launched up and into the overall will of God. We will begin to understand and fellowship with "the what, the why, the way and the who" of the Lord Jesus Christ. His priorities will become ours; His thoughts will become ours; His passions will become ours. We will see through His eyes because He has enlightened our eyes, and in His light we will see more light.

By faith we are learning to follow Him and flow with Him. Matthew 9:38 says to beseech the Lord of the harvest to send forth laborers into His harvest field. Jesus is the greatest farmer and harvester in the universe, and He has a particular crop. He planted the seed of His life and His obedience. Now He is looking for that dearest of harvests, the precious fruit of the earth. He is the only One who could have planted such a seed, therefore, He is the only One who knows how to bring in the harvest from it. And harvest it He will. And harvest it YOU will as you follow on to know Him and His ways.

John 4:35-36 says, "Do you not say, 'There are still four months and then comes the harvest?' Behold, I say to you, lift up your eyes and look at the fields, for they are already white for harvest!" When Jesus said this, did the people around Him strain to see the fields on the outskirts of the city? If they did, they still would not have seen what Jesus was seeing—it takes eyes that see the way Jesus sees. This type of vision is not that of a lowly, carnal, earthbound nature. We must *lift up* to see what He sees. When we pray the Ephesians prayer, we are *lifted up out of our mental reasonings, out of ourselves, out of our ways and into His ways.* The Ephesians prayer will launch you up and out by faith to see the harvest. You will see *His* harvest, and *you will see the way He sees.*

Isn't it interesting that the Bible always describes

harvest fields as *white?* Why is that? It's because the harvest of the world is ready and awaits only the laborers be sent to it. The laborers of the last-day harvest are the company of present-day *saints!* Folks, that's you and me! Ephesians 1:22-23 declares, "...He put all things under His feet, and gave Him to be head over all things *to the church, which is His body, the fullness of Him who fills all in all."*

The mighty Ephesians prayer culminates and has the audacity and the authority to name and define what happens when the saints move collectively in this way. The Bible calls us the very *"body of Christ"* and further exclaims that we are the very *"fullness of Him that shall fill all in [and through] all."* As we are filled with His revelation and propelled by His power and presence, we carry His fullness within *us* to *all* the people of the earth. Hallelujah!

We collectively become the very fullness of the Godhead in a bodily form, in the form of the body of Christ. We become couriers and carriers—a veritable *vehicle*—of the very presence of God. The body of Christ becomes the vehicle that delivers the Word of God and the power of God to the world. That same body of Christ is then the very vehicle that the saints climb into and are translated in to meet Him at His soon coming. The Spirit-Filled Life Bible defines the word *fullness* that is presented in Ephesians 1:23. The "word wealth" of this Bible defines the *fullness* of Him as a "ship having a full crew and a full cargo." Supreme, amazing awesomeness!

So pray the Ephesians prayer! Get on board! Get into that ship—the fellow**ship** of the saints. Get moving! Experience revelation of who you are and what you are called to do. Let the revelation bring an enduement of power, a demonstration of that which you now believe. Watch that revelation and demonstration *place you* within the body of Christ and allow you to experience the absolute fullness of Him that shall fill you and shall fill all around you. Board that ship of glory! Let it take you to a revelation of who you are. Let it take you to the lost. Then ultimately—that fullness, that body, that vehicle, that ship—will take you and all of us to meet Him.

The answer and or fulfillment of praying the Ephesians prayer **is** that the individual saint arises and does the will of God. *The saint who prays this prayer shall discover himself or herself to be the very answer to this prayer as these saints become the very fullness of Him that shall fill all in all!*

CHAPTER 7

THE **BIBLE** AND **THE HOLY SPIRIT** IN PRAYER

No matter what some folks might think, the amount of time spent praying is not at all the bottom line of productive prayer. Pure and simple, the most important elements of prayer are faith and the Word of God.

In fact, there is no effectual prayer apart from faith and God's Word. Why? Because faith does not come through prayer; faith comes by hearing and hearing by the Word of God.

No wonder. God's Word *is* His will. First John 5:14-15 says, "This is the confidence that we have in Him, that, if we ask any thing according to His will, He heareth us: And if we know that He hear us, whatsoever we ask, we know that we have the petitions that we desired of Him" (KJV). John 15:7-8 says, "If ye abide in me, and my words abide in you, ye shall ask what ye will, and it shall be done unto you" (KJV). Proverbs 28:9 tells us, "He that turneth away his ear from hearing the law, even his prayer shall be an abomination" (KJV).

The Bible says that God the Father has exalted His

Word even above His own name. That says a lot. There are many spirits in the world and none without signification. Yet, we want to follow the spirit who is holy and the spirit who is of God—*the Holy Spirit.* There is only one place we can learn to follow the Spirit of God and that's through the Word of God.

John 15:26 says, "When the Helper comes, the Spirit of Truth, He will lead and guide us through all the Truth ...." This verse is telling us that contextually and chronologically if we follow the Spirit of God through the truth of God's Word, then in the place of prayer we will be able to follow the Spirit of God as He shows us "things to come" (John 16:13) not written in the Word of God. *In other words, if we will allow the Spirit of God to lead and guide us through the Word of God,* **then we can follow Him in prayer.**

Here's another way to explain it. If we can find a way to *invite* or *allow* the Spirit of God to lead and guide us—with full liberty and full expression to highlight, reveal, connect, explain, declare and disclose scriptures—we'll be looking good. The sum total of that supernatural revelation will equip us when we go to prayer. Our hearts will have been trained by His leadings through the Word. Our hearts will be a safe and effectual guide harnessed to the bit of the Word by the mouth of the Holy Ghost.

Let us say it again yet another way. If we have learned to study the Word of God with the "lamp of the Holy Ghost" that allows Him to enlighten scriptures and make them real to us, then—and only then—can we follow Him into the world of the spirit called prayer. In this world of the spirit called prayer, He shall show us things to come that are not written in the Bible, but are just as much the plan of God as those things written in black and white and bound with leather. Only then is our heart a safe and worthy guide to read the scroll of old in accordance with Ephesians 2:10, "taking paths predestined before the foundation of the world." *The same Spirit who "bears witness" to us of scriptures as we read them is the same Spirit who shall lead and guide us in prayer and "bear witness" to people, subjects, places, nations and situations of urgency when we pray.*

A FLIPPIN EXAMPLE

Awhile back I went to preach in Flippin, Arkansas. Oh yeah. Believe me, the word *Flippin* is not in the Bible anywhere. I even joked with the pastor there. "So, are you the Flippin pastor?" I asked. "How is your Flippin church doing?" I also inquired. Or, "How are the Flippin deacons?" Isn't that awesome? Sometimes I wonder if the Lord leads me places just so I can get some good jokes. Awesome. I am wondering if the Lord will ever lead me to Toadsuck, Arkansas. Talk about preaching to every creature.

Again, *Flippin* is not written in the Bible. How then did I know on the inside of me that it was right to go to Flippin to preach? How was I sure that my travels to Flippin would be within the will of God for me? I knew because I have followed the Holy Spirit through the Word of God and learned His voice, His ways, His character, His nature and the *witness* of His Spirit. So when the opportunity of going to Flippin came before me, the Holy Spirit rose up and bore witness to this opportunity the same way He rises up and bears witness to scriptures when I read them.

"Wow!" you say. "He bears witness, huh? Well,

what does that mean? And how do you get this 'bear witnessing thing' to happen?"

I am so glad you asked.

Turn to John 15:7-8 in your Bible. You can highlight scripture as we go. This scripture actually makes a startling point and says:

John 15:7-8

"If you abide in Me, and My words abide in you, you will ask what you desire, and it shall be done for you. By this My Father is glorified, that you bear much fruit; so you will be My disciples."

What an amazing statement. This scripture promises if you *abide* in Him and His Words *abide* in you, you will ask what **you** desire and it shall be done for you. Wow! Ask what you desire, and it will actually get done for you. Can it get any better?

So many Christians spend so much time praying. But even after racking up the hours in prayer, too often they don't know what they're praying about or what they're requesting. So I wonder: *How then will they recognize the answer when it shows up?* Trouble is, so many people are praying and asking amiss, which is why they're not getting what they petitioned for in prayer. That's sad. *But*, this amazing scripture gives us a clue on how to pray correctly.

Essentially, you've got to get this "abiding deal" happening. "If you **abide** in Me and My Words **abide** in you," He said, "...you can ask *whatever you desire*." See, when this **abiding** thing starts happening, God will begin to conform, mold and shape your desires to match His. As His Word begins to truly **abide** in you, a hunger for Him and the things of righteousness—a hunger not even of yourself—will arise in you for Him. A ravenous appetite for the things of God will begin to consume you and gobble up desires for things not of Him.

Incoming news flash! Quit trying to stop sinning! There's just no better way to say it—give it up! Get the abiding thing happening instead. Matthew 1:21 says, "Thou shalt call His name Jesus for He shall save *His own people* from their sins."

Jesus didn't just take your sins when He died on the Cross, He *became sin* for you that you in turn would not just give up a few sins, but that *you would literally become the righteousness of God in Christ.* So quit trying to fight your way out of sin. Let the Lord sort through that for you. Instead, you just focus on abiding and watch your desires change.

The Lord will begin to paint a picture of His plan and purpose for your life. As you *abide in Him,* **He** will show you—**you**! He will prompt in you His ultimate plan for you. As He does, **those desires become the blueprint of what He has called you to do.**

THE BEAUTY OF 'ABIDING'

Watch out for what *abiding* will do! For example, look what happened to sick people who hung around Jesus. Looking through the Gospels, we see people always had a need when they went to Jesus. The need brought them, and He met the need. But in the process people got to know the "Need Meeter," and they came to know the tender nature of their heavenly

Father. They came to know the One who was stricken, sickened and marred for them even to the point of death so they could experience healing. He healed them and then let them go run and play. He knows how to draw His children and love them and **even help them to love Him.**

Now again, John 15:7-8 tells us that if we abide in Him and His words abide in us, we shall ask what we desire and it shall be done for us. By this our Father is glorified that we shall bear much fruit, so shall we be His disciples.

This verse tells us there's definitely a way to pray that actually glorifies the Lord, causes us to be fruitful and establishes us as disciples. This verse says there's a way to pray that causes the glory of the Lord to manifest. There is a way to pray that causes us to bring in the precious peoples of the harvest and exude His peace, love, power and presence. There's a way to pray that draws us to the Word of God and showcases the Word of God causing us to fall in love with it. There's a way to pray wherein the Holy Spirit cannot communicate apart from the words of God; it lets us feel the fabric of the Word, sense the breeze of which way the Word is blowing and know the personality of the One speaking. There's a way to pray that teaches us how to "speak" the language of God. As we speak any language, we must first learn the words before speaking them in the context of that language.

There's a way to pray that leads us to the Word of God and then that very Word of God catapults us back into prayer. There's a way to pray that creates a divine relationship between the Word of God and prayer. This is an amazing relationship where we cannot tell the difference between our times of prayer and our Bible study time. As we dive into His written words, those scriptures inspire hunger, desire, questions, ideas, thoughts and plans that we must discuss with Him. We become disciples one by one. And there's a way to pray that is actually effectual where we actually receive answers to our prayers and come away having truly fellowshipped with the living God.

So, how do we get this "abiding thing" happening? Where can I buy an "abider?" It sounds like the "ab roller" or the "ab lounge" I saw on the Home Shopping Network. Does it come with a warranty? Actually, it does!

Let's let the Word of God show us what abiding in God's Word really is and how to do it:

1 John 2:27

"But the anointing which *you* have received from Him *abides* in *you,* and *you* do not need that anyone teach *you;* but as the same anointing teaches *you* concerning all things, and is true, and is not a lie, and just as it has taught *you, you* will *abide* in Him."

First of all, this scripture tells us that each born-again believer has received an anointing. The way the word *anointing* is used here, it is the Greek word *charisma* and means an "unction." Webster's definition of the word *unction* pretty much describes its *function. Unction* is an anointing, the shedding of a divine influence upon a person, an affected earnestness and fervor. Yet another definition is a peace and a soothing.

If you are born again, this verse tells you that *you* have an *unction* or *anointing* of the Holy Spirit. Look at how many times this verse says the word *you.* It does not say "only the woman who wrote the book you're reading has an anointing." It does not say "only your favorite preacher has an anointing." It does not say that "the group of ladies who pray in your church and pray a lot more than you do have an anointing." Now all of these people do have an unction and an anointing, but this verse says *you have an anointing!*

If you have asked Jesus into your heart—whether you feel like it or not—you have an unction of the Holy Spirit. You, who may have cussed last night or yelled at your wife this morning, simply repent because you still have an unction of the Holy Spirit of God on the inside of *you—you—you—you!*

You have anointing, and *you* have divine influence from the Holy Spirit. By faith, He is influencing which way **you** go, and He *is* leading **you** to do what is right. This unction or witness of the Holy Spirit is even teaching **you** what the Holy Ghost is like. Brother and Sister, **you** are under the influence—thank God!

As you continue **to believe it**, you'll be influenced by the Spirit of God in every area of life. You will have an urgency about what He does and doesn't want you to do, and you will have a sudden fervor or urgency about situations. I can't necessarily explain it, but this or that will just seem right; there will be an earnestness and or sudden peace or expectancy about the matter. There will be a divine red light or green light on the inside of you regarding situations, people and decisions.

This verse goes on to say:

1 John 2:27

"But the anointing which you have received from

Him **abides** in you, and you do not need that anyone teach you; but as the same anointing teaches you concerning all things, and is true, and is not a lie, and just as it has taught you, you will **abide** in Him."

Hey, here's that "abiding thing" again! So here's a good idea: How about we let the Word of God interpret and define the word *abiding* for us: " ... but as *the same anointing teaches you* concerning all things, and is true, and is not a lie, and *just as it has taught* you, you will **abide** in Him."

This verse tells us if we will allow the Holy Spirit to *teach us*, we will *abide* in the Lord. The Holy Spirit was sent to teach us the Word of God, which means He will declare, disclose and transmit God's purposes and power to us. But the primary way He will teach us is through the Word of God. Again, as we allow Him to teach us the Word of God, His words will begin to *abide* in our hearts.

So how does He teach us the Word anyway? Will He teach us through ministers and pastors? Yes, a thousand times yes. Ephesians 4:8-12 tells us that God has given us *gifts* called apostles, prophets, evangelists, pastors and teachers for the equipping and perfecting of the saints. God the Father gave these precious ministry gifts to us, and He will never execute His plans without the fivefold ministers' affects in our lives. He has set ministers in the body as it has so pleased Him.

My opinion is that probably 20 percent of direction, confirmation and instruction will come to you through ministry. But again my opinion is that about 80 percent of what you hear from God will come directly to you through your own personal study of God's Word and your prayer time. Now, on the flip side, let me say that Christians who spend a lot of time with God, but never hook up with a pastor, will conversely find something is always a little bit dip wad. Or, in other words, nothing seems to ever quite fit or work right. You see, they might have the 80 percent personal devotion down, but again, apart from the ministry gifts, everything they do will be about 20 percent dip wad. Please also consider that these percentages do not even begin to reflect the amount of influence that flowing in a local church with your brothers and sisters will afford. There is no "doing the will of God" apart from being in fellowship with the saints of God. The Lord has deemed the collection of the saints as His personal body, and a member of the body cannot survive apart from vital connection to His body—the Church.

If you truly follow the Holy Spirit through the Word of God and effectually in prayer, you'll never be led away from the fellowship of the saints. The Spirit of God will always lead you to have fellowship with the saints, and He will always lead you to a church and to a pastor. The plan of God for your life always involves participation in the body of Christ.

I also believe—and it's born out in scripture—that the office of the pastor offers a safe haven for prayer. (We are preparing another book on praying for your pastor—a key to finding your place in the body of Christ. The book is another teaching altogether, but I wanted to reference it here to establish what makes for effectual prayer.) So, yes, the Holy Spirit will teach us through the ministry gifts. These gifts are a divine supplement, and without them no saint can effectually serve God. Remember, *if we can get the*

Holy Spirit to teach us, we will abide in Him—and so shall we have His desires, bear His fruit, be His disciples, and glorify Him.

THE PRIMARY WAY SAINTS ARE TAUGHT

Let's turn to the book of 1 John and consider the primary way the Lord will teach each and every saint.

1 John 5:6

"This is he that came by water and blood, even Jesus Christ; not by water only, but by water and blood. ... ***And it is the Spirit that beareth witness, because the Spirit is truth.***"

Notice! It is the Spirit who *bears witness* because the Spirit is truth. The scripture gives another name of the Holy Spirit called the *Spirit of Truth*. Or, John 17:17 says, "Thy word is truth." Thus, *He is the Spirit of the Word.* Hallelujah! This scripture teaches us that He *bears witness* to the *truth* or to the *Word.*

How do we abide in Him and His words abide in us? According to 1 John 2:27, we do so *if we allow the Holy Spirit to teach us His Word.* How does He teach us? When we read His Word, the Spirit of Truth—that unction or witness we have—**will arise on the inside of us and begin to bear witness to specific scriptures, passages, isolated words, entire contexts and themes of the Bible.**

The Holy Spirit or Spirit of Truth will also **bear witness** in your spirit or heart. For instance, to bear witness to a scripture means that the inward unction and anointing of the Holy Spirit will quicken you as you read your Bible. *The Holy Spirit will seize upon a scripture and suddenly "highlight" it to your heart.* In fact, it may seem to leap from the page at you. One person said that as the Holy Ghost quickens scriptures, it seems as though an entire passage stands up on the page and begins to leap and twirl. *Scriptures will seem as though they are waving their hands and saying, "Hey, over here! Your healing is right here! Your answer is right here! Turn aside and see this great thing!* (In the Old Testament, when God called Moses, it said Moses saw a bush that was burning, and yet, the bush was not consumed. Moses said, "I will turn aside and see this great thing." As you follow the scriptures today, you can have greater experiences in God, even greater than what Moses had!)

Proverbs 1:20 says, "Wisdom cries aloud outside, she raises her voice in the open squares!" Friend, God is not hiding your blessings. So just let the Holy Ghost lead and teach you the Word. You'll find that the blessings have been trying to chase you down. Encouragement, enlightenment, tangible peace and healing for your body and mind—are all available 24 hours a day. Watch the passages come alive with answers—nothing is impossible, and every possible need and situation has an answer. Hallelujah!

What a personal and wondrous thing. So many people seek for an outward sign, a fleece if you will. They talk to God like this: "If You will make it rain for five days in a row, then I will know it is Your will for me to go to Africa." No, no! That is not how God will speak to you; He is a Spirit, and He will speak to *your spirit.*

Think how miraculous and intimate that is. You are reading your Bible and all of the sudden, your eyes land upon a scripture. Perhaps it seems to be a scripture that has nothing to do with your situation. Yet as you read it, it helps you. Perhaps you're reading

Hebrews 13:5 and your eyes fall upon the last part of the verse, "I will never leave thee, nor forsake thee." These are the words of Jesus. Suddenly that portion of verse comes alive to you; peace and comfort arise in your heart. You feel tension leave your back. For lack of a better term—man, that scripture just really blessed you.

The Bible says in John 1:14 that Jesus is the Word made flesh. In other words, when you read a scripture and the Holy Spirit quickens it to you, it's like you're sitting with the risen Savior and He's speaking personally to you. Hey, think about it. Jesus just spoke to you! Your Bible is God talking to you. My Bible is God talking to me. Glory!

CHAPTER 8

THE EPHESIANS **PRAYER GLASSES**

Get ready to ruuummmble. I mean, reeeaaad your Bible. Here goes. John 15:7-8 tells us, "If you abide in Me, and My words abide in you, you will ask what you desire, and it shall be done for you. By this my Father is glorified, that you bear much fruit; so you will be my disciples." First John 2:27 defines *abiding* as allowing the anointing and or the unction of the Holy Spirit to "teach us" the Word of God. First John 5:6 says the Holy Spirit teaches us the Word of God by the action of "bearing witness" to scriptures. The number one way the Christian is to be led is by the *inward witness* of the Holy Spirit.

Now let me ask this. How do we get in position for the Holy Spirit to bear witness to the scriptures? What can we do to cause the Word of God to come alive and the voice of the Lord to resound loud and clear? I'll tell you. **You've got to put on your glasses—your Ephesians prayer glasses!**

Before I read my Bible—every time I read my Bible—I put on my reading glasses, *my Ephesians prayer glasses*. How? Like this. I place my hand on my Bible before I even open its pages and pray the prayer found in Ephesians 1:17-23. I pray it from my heart; I mean every word of it.

Here's how I talk to the Lord about it: "Father, I'm getting ready to read my Bible, and so I thank You that my Bible is Jesus speaking to me. I thank You, Father, I do not read this Bible after familiarity or as a form of works. I read my Bible and pray this Ephesians prayer believing as I open its pages that You will speak to me.

"You said if I ask anything in accordance with Your will that You hear me. I believe that, and I have a request. I ask, as Paul the apostle prayed for the Ephesians, that You would grant to me the spirit of wisdom and revelation in the knowledge of You. I ask that today as I am reading my Bible that the Spirit of wisdom and revelation would speak to me! I ask that the eyes of my heart would be enlightened and that I would come to know the hope of Your calling and the riches of your glorious inheritance on the inside of me.

"I ask that today I would come to know more by experience the exceeding greatness of your power according to the working of Your power, which You wrought in Christ when you raised Jesus from the dead and seated Him at your right hand in the heavenlies. You seated Jesus far above all principalities, powers, might and dominion and every name that is named both now and in the ages to come. I thank You, Father, that You have put all things under His feet and given Jesus to be the head of the Church, which is His body, the fullness of Him who fills all in all. I thank You for speaking to me. Father, I hear Your voice, and I know You!"

Then I open my Bible, preferably starting in the New Testament, and I begin to read—read, read, read like I'm mowing grass. One word after the other, paragraph after paragraph, left to right and back and forth letting the Word of God that's quick and alive do the talking. Just read.

One time a friend and I went to a 3-D movie about how 3-D movies are made—go figure. As we walked into the theater, an usher handed us a strange pair of glasses—big white cardboard glasses with red and green lenses. How very strange and embarrassing. We took the glasses and balanced them with our mega-movie meals (amazingly just a quarter more). The deal included a silo of soda, a barrel of popcorn and a chocolate bar the size of the raft they found Tom Hanks on in *Castaway*.

Soon after the movie began, strange things began to happen. Things seemed to POP out of the screen at us. If you peeked around the glasses, things just looked flat and a little odd. But once those glasses were on, we were suddenly immersed in a movie that seemed to engulf and surround us. It was as if we became a part of that movie.

At one point these strange little shapes looked like stars floating off the screen toward us. I looked at my friend to comment, but he was too busy reaching out to grab them. He looked like he had lost his mind. As I turned back to the screen, there was a cartoon robot—actually, a big gray animated metal-looking robot. This robot moved around the screen and then those big metal arms started to reach out to the audience. I was trying to look cool and drink my 40 gallons of soda, but those arms kept coming toward me. Those arms reached so far out that it looked like that robot was touching my face. I lost my cool. I dropped my soda—and 13 people drowned. It was the first ever tsunami warning issued for the southern portions of Tulsa, Oklahoma.

My dignity was waiting for me in the parking lot I yelled so loud. As we walked out of the theater, I asked my friend, "Did you see that robot thing reach out and touch me? Of all the people in the theater, can you believe it reached out for me?"

"It didn't reach out for you! It reached out for me!" my friend looked back and said.

Those glasses caused the images on the screen to look as though they had come alive! Those glasses made what we were looking at reach out to us, involve us and speak individually to each of us.

Guess what? When you have on your Ephesians prayer glasses, the Word of God will look mighty different as well. Before the Word may have seemed like a bunch of pages lying flat in a book on your kitchen table. The words and phrases may have seemed jumbled and odd, but as you put on those glasses suddenly the Word of God becomes 3-D.

Passages will jump out at you. Scenarios of Jesus healing the sick or speaking to the disciples will surround you and pull you in. You become a part of the picture. You read the book of Acts and see the apostles healing the masses, and suddenly, the apostles disappear as you see yourself healing the masses in His glorious name. Scriptures of Jesus healing people jump out at you.

Suppose as you leave your house today, you see a person in a wheelchair and your hands begin to burn and tingle as you recall those scriptures. You remember the scripture in Mark 16:17 that says, "These signs shall follow them that believe...they shall lay hands on the sick and they shall recover." So you politely, yet boldly, approach the person in the wheelchair asking if you can pray for him or her because the will of God is coming alive to you. You are becoming a fulfillment of the very scriptures you've been reading. You look and act like the disciples did because you're now abiding in His words and His words are abiding in you.

You're watching the fulfillment of John 15:7-8, which says "so will you be My disciples." You have become the fulfillment—you have become the disciple. Or, perhaps you become intrigued with Phillip the evangelist or stirred by the passage where Jesus called the little children to Himself. *Find yourself in God's Word—I promise you are in there!* You're there—in heaven's atmosphere, where its victory, love and possibilities encompass you. You sit with the Lord on the mount. You read the love passage in 1 Corinthians 13 and see yourself moving in realms of forgiveness and mercy you've never known before.

Just like my friend reaching out to those images as they came toward him from the movie screen, the Word will begin to impact you and *then your outward actions will change.* People will say, "Why is he acting like that? Why is she being so kind to us? Why won't he or she gossip?"Your actions are changing because you are seeing something others don't see. Your Ephesians glasses are causing you to clearly see the unseen realm so that your actions are impacted by a raw faith emanating from the Word.

Just like that robot, something of the scriptures will begin to paint a portrait showing who you are and what you are called to do—and in that portrait will be the people to whom you are called. Even though the scriptures were written thousands of years ago by the power of the Holy Spirit, they come alive and reach out to touch you individually. Remember, the 3-D image on the movie screen reached out and grabbed not only me, but also my friend. The glasses made all the difference. The Word of God is so alive, and the scriptures have the ability to speak to anyone, to everyone and to any situation throughout time and eternity. Glory to God! Get your glasses on!

TOOLS FOR PRAYER

To get started, here's what you'll need:

1. Bible. Get one you like. Some will get a King James Version. If you do, get ready for a lot of "thees" and "thous" as personal pronouns. Also, there will be a lot of "ths" at the end of words. I prefer the New King James Bible—it is an accurate enough translation without drowning readers in the proper English of ancient times. Some people like a translation called The Living Bible. My opinion (that's all it is—an opinion) is that The Living Bible is OK and fun, but it's not so accurate to the original Greek. I like a pretty tight translation. When you let the Holy Spirit lead you through the scriptures, you'll want to stay as close to the original Greek as possible. But get whatever Bible floats your boat.

Second Peter 1:21 tells us, "...prophecy never came by the will of man, but holy men of God spoke as they were moved by the Holy Spirit." The Bible is a miracle—it's a supernatural book. Men of old spoke as the Holy Ghost moved upon them, and that's why we want our translation as close as possible. The words that were spoken and or written were chosen for a reason. To find out their pure meaning is to unleash their full punch and ability to move supernaturally in your life. Many consider the The New American Standard Bible as the most accurate translation.

It's also important to get a Bible you can write in and mark up with yellow, red, blue, green, pink and orange highlights. Get a Bible where you feel free to attach paper clips, staples, 2-by-4s, caulking and masking tape. Get a Bible you can drip mustard on while reading. Your Bible isn't even broken in if there's not a coffee stain in the Gospels somewhere. Make sure there's a chai tea latte drop somewhere around Philippians 4:19 that says, "My God shall supply all your needs according to His riches in glory by Christ Jesus!"

Folks, throw Grandma's coffee table Bible back on the coffee table. "But it has the names of all our dead relatives in it," you say, "and Baby John's first teeth and hair are in that Bible. Several body parts are in the index." OK, fine! Put that Bible back on the coffee table and save its contents in case you ever want to clone Baby John. But don't use it to study!

2. Ephesians Prayer Glasses. Pray with them on as outlined in previous paragraphs of instruction. Pray Ephesians 1:17-23 over yourself word for word and mean it, and pray it every time you open the Bible to read God's Word. This is called putting on your Ephesians prayer glasses, and you need them on every single time you read. Just because you had them on last time doesn't mean they're on this time. You cannot do without your reading glasses because you need to read by faith, and you must read by faith because Hebrews 11 tells us faith pleases God. Make sure that you never approach the Bible out of familiarity, works, presumption, tradition, religion or apathy.

3. Pen.

4. Notebook or Journal. Dude, my opinion is to go get a *nice* journal and use it only for writing notes during Bible study and prayer time. Get one that you'll respect. Make it leather with a cowboy on it or pink velvet with fur and maybe Martha Stewart's picture on it. I don't know. Get whatever you like. But get a nice one because you're going to write down what you believe the Lord has been quickening and highlighting to you. So this is a pretty important journal!

The best journal I ever found was for a child who loved to pray. This journal had like weird 3-D laminate on the cover of these cool old-school aliens. When you tilted the journal different ways the alien would either come out of or go back into his spaceship. The clerk who rang me up seemed to be, generally speaking, a very "unimpressed" artsy book person. At first he didn't speak to me or even smile. However, upon viewing the journal I was purchasing, he hesitated and a bit of expression showed on his face, interest I think. I thought, *Oh my, is he going to speak to me? What's happening?*

He looked at me; I held my breath. And he said, "This is a really cool journal!" My, my, I felt like Moses had just confirmed my decision to purchase this journal. Wow!

Now, *let's get started!*

Put your hand on your Bible.

Pray out loud the prayer found in Ephesians 1:17-23. Pray the entire prayer just as it is in your Bible—even if you don't understand it all. Just pray it and mean it. Pray all the way from verse 17 to verse 23. You don't have to embellish it, and even if you do, purpose to finish the whole prayer as it is.

Now open your Bible to the New Testament, preferably the Epistles—those "books" in between the Gospels and the book of Revelations—and start reading!

Write down scriptures as they:

1. Jump out at you.

2. Come alive and bless you.

3. Inspire a question to arise to you.

4. Prompt you and cause correction.

5. Intrigue you, provoke you, seem interesting to you and make you want to research or investigate.

In other words, write down scriptures that jump out at you. Write down passages that jump out at you. Write down words that jump out at you, puzzle you, intrigue you and/or bless you. Then write down the location of the scripture and passage. Whew, but that's a lot of writing. So what? It's the Word of God for goodness sake. These are God's words to you, and they are worthy of writing.

Second Timothy 2:15 says, "**Study** to shew thyself approved unto God, a **workman** that needeth not to be ashamed, rightly dividing the word of truth." See, there is some **study** and **work** involved. Psalm 45:1 says, "My tongue is (as) the pen of a ready writer."

I dare you! I dare you to poise your pen ready in faith that God is going to speak to you. Lift your pen as an act of faith. Write the scripture or passage that is being highlighted to you. Then, I double-dog dare you to write down what you believe God is speaking to you about that scripture or passage. As you dare to believe and write in faith, God will take a hold of that pen. He will overflow your heart with His faith, His words, His thoughts and His plans and purposes. Your heart and your journal will fill with God's attitude and His victory. Oppression will be swallowed up by robust faith that will vanquish the greatest of impossibilities, lies and obstacles.

You will begin to fellowship with the **mind-set** of the Lord. You will begin to sense His leadings and His ways. You will begin to think like He does. His preferences will become yours, His priorities your own. After all, you are abiding in His Word, and His Words are abiding in you. You are conforming to His image, and His desires are becoming yours. So you ask what you will, and it's done for you because you are asking what He wills. **You can barely tell the difference between His heartbeat and yours.**

As you dare to believe and write in faith, God will overflow you, and then He will flow out to others through you. As you write down those scriptures and then in even more robust faith daringly write what you believe the Lord is saying to you about those scriptures, **the Father will be glorified.** You will bear fruit, and greatest of all, **you will become His disciple.** That pen will become as the tongue, the leading or the voice of God to you.

God will speak through the pen that is ready to write!
Dip that quill into the well of faith.
God will supply the ink of His plans and purposes.
We are His living epistles,
Known and read of all men.
He is writing on the tablet of our hearts!

CHAPTER 9

RUBBER-MEETS-THE-ROAD EXAMPLES OF HOW PRAYER WORKS

Life has begun to change for you, as you've been receiving personal instruction from the Holy Spirit.

You've been praying the Ephesians prayer out loud over yourself. You're opening your Bible to the New Testament daring to see what the Holy Spirit quickens and highlights to you. In accordance with John 15:7-8, you're letting the Holy Spirit teach you the Word, and you're recognizing how the Holy Spirit will bear witness.

As you've been yielding to the action of the Holy Spirit's witness, you're learning to follow the inward witness (1 John 2:27). The Holy Spirit will *teach you* the truth, and thus, teach you all things. First John 5:6 says, "And it is the Spirit Who bears witness, because the Spirit is Truth." Of course, that means the Holy Spirit will *bear witness* first and foremost to the truth of God's Word.

The Holy Spirit will bear witness to scriptures that will help you build your life and calling. Then, as that inward witness gets stronger, you'll be led regarding daily living—decisions, events, opportunities and people vital to your life. This is earthshakingly vital to your future! Even though these specifics are not literally named or labeled in the Bible, they are yet destined as the plan of God for your life as though written in stone before the foundations of the universe.

It's so critical that you learn to follow the **inward witness through God's Word, through prayer and through daily living.** The Holy Spirit holds the divine and supernatural combination to victory and success in every situation. And if you stick with Him, He'll impart it to you one witness at a time.

'RATS! I'VE GOT TO WALK IN LOVE'

OK, ready for some examples? Here's a good one. Let's say I open my Bible—Bible roulette style—and pick a book of the Bible, any book. *Voil`a!* Here's one in 1 Corinthians, and it looks as good as any. So I decide: *Guess I'll start reading around Chapter 12.*

So I begin to read like I'm mowing the lawn—back and forth, back and forth my eyes move over line upon line. I'm reading in raw faith, watching and waiting for that inward witness. It's pretty uneventful so far, but I forge ahead continuing to read. In obedience and under the influence of the Ephesians prayer my eyes press forward; it's maybe even not so exciting until I hit Chapter 13. Oh wow!

First Corinthians 13:4-8 says, "Love suffers long and is kind; love does not envy; love does not parade itself, is not puffed up; does not behave rudely, does not seek its own, is not provoked, thinks no evil; does not rejoice in iniquity, but rejoices in the truth; bears all things, believes all things, hopes all things, endures all things. Love never fails… " (KJV).

I write down this scripture as it jumps out to me. Ouch! It's kind of a rebuke, but it's a good rebuke. There is a peace and a good clean feeling in my belly as I acknowledge it.

Yikes! I write down the scripture: "Love … is kind."

Kind? (Boy, am I in trouble.)

I dare to write down what I feel the Holy Spirit is saying to me about the scripture—about being kind. I write, "I guess it means if someone is driving 40 mph in a 50-mph zone that I should not display a moronic, cross-eyed stare when I pass them."

Hmmm, yes, good note to self. I adjust and consecrate my heart. I purpose to be kind when I am driving.

Even if someone is on a cell phone, or even if a soccer mom tries to drive over me, I purpose to be kind. Even if a person tailgates my car so closely I can see from my rearview mirror that he or she has something stuck in his or her teeth, I will purpose to be kind. Or even if those stupid...ooops...I better go back and look at that scripture again and consecrate again. Practice makes perfect; I am *exercising* myself unto godliness.

First Timothy 4:7-8 teaches us, "…**exercise** yourself toward godliness. For bodily exercise profits a little, but godliness is profitable for all things…." (Let's face it. You have to stick with exercising for a while before you can see permanent changes. In the love department, I am a work in progress and so are you.)

Oh dear, that passage in 1Corinthians goes on to say, "Love ... does not behave rudely." Oh well, I wrote down the word *rude* on my paper before I even read it in the Bible. Looks like I am really on the right frequency.

Oh, no! What does that next part say? Oh dear, the Holy Spirit is bearing witness to this part of the scripture too! Rats! It says " ... love is not provoked, it thinks no evil...." Well, obviously Jesus never worked at my job with Cruelle De Vil. She is the spawn of Satan. She gossips about me, persecutes me, and she doesn't walk in any kind of integrity. The woman takes credit for my ideas and sugar talks the boss! By the way, these are her *good points!*

Or you could be thinking: *Jesus was never married, so He has no idea how bad it could be with my ex-wife. She is trying to keep me from my kids—she even lies to them about me. She's trying to use the courts to prevent my visitation rights. I wasn't a Christian when we were married, or at least I was not behaving like a Christian. So I guess I deserve whatever she dishes out.*

Or worse beyond belief, maybe you're thinking: *My husband sexually abused my children for 10 years before I knew or could face what was happening.*

Yet, it doesn't matter what situation, circumstance or personality you face. Here's the truth: The Bible doesn't promise that bad situations won't arise. However, as we walk with the Lord led by His Spirit and following that inward witness, our lives will sidestep much havoc, death, tribulation and destruction. The inward witness will warn us before we get into situations that could produce harm. That is great victory right there! However, for those difficult situations that do still happen or have already happened—and for those things that we did in the past—we have instruction from the Word of God to help us *always triumph* in every situation.

First Corinthians 13:5 in The Amplified Bible tells us that, "love is not easily provoked" and "love believes the best of every person." These verses are not talking about *natural human* love or a love that is based on your five senses or feelings. Natural human love says, "If you spit on me, then I will spit on you." That's the concept of the Old Testament that says "an eye for an eye and a tooth for a tooth." That's not the case here. First Corinthians 13:5 is telling you what you *can do* now that you are a born-again Christian. This passage is a **mirror** to you—a mirror of truth. It's showing you a reflection of what's in you.

It's not "yelling at you and shaming you for not displaying the love of God." This passage is a mirror showing you the truth that the love of God has been shed abroad in your heart by the Holy Ghost. By faith you are well able to tap in to the love of God. You can love and forgive other people, and you can allow others to experience the love of God. You can also love and forgive yourself. You can allow yourself to know the love that your heavenly Father has for you!

There's no doubt about it, *we cannot do this in our own strength or natural ability.* But as we acknowledge **the scriptures; they** release the power of God, the love of God, the forgiveness of God and **His ability** within us to even be a "doer of the Word."

Romans 5:5 says, "The love of God is shed abroad in our hearts by the Holy Ghost which is given unto us." God has deposited His love in our hearts so we must use this precious commodity. We must use His love to believe the best about our enemies. We must use His love to escape being provoked by evil. We must use His love to love our enemies—to forgive a person or an act that could never be forgiven with natural love. We must let His love in us loose and free us from bitterness.

So I write down that scripture that says, "Love is not provoked" and "love believes the best." As I do the Holy Ghost then prompts me to remember something Jesus said on the Cross. Luke 23:34 quotes Jesus saying, "Father, forgive them, for they do not know what they do."

If people do something evil to us, the Bible instructs us that they are "blind" to the evil or essentially they do not realize what they're actually doing. This does not justify their actions, but if we walk in the truths of the Bible, we'll be shielded from the negative effects of their actions. Acting in line with the scriptures will line us up—provide guardrails—and enable to keep us on the road to absolute victory and fulfillment in every area of life.

So after writing down the scripture, I write down what I believe the Holy Spirit is saying to me about that scripture. I write, "Thank You, Father, I believe the Bible is God speaking to me. Since Your Word says that 'I am not to be provoked,' by faith I am not provoked or angry with these people. By faith I forgive them. Thank You, Father, that faith is not a feeling, but faith is an action. So I thank You, Lord, that if I forgive these people by faith and by my actions, then feelings of forgiveness will follow."

FORGIVING EVEN YOURSELF

Here is another example of the-worst-it-could-possibly-be scenario. Say you were an alcoholic all your life, and your children were "marred." Perhaps your marriage and career were ruined. Or, perhaps nobody was "greatly harmed in the making of your life." Still, because you may not have been a Christian all your life, there may be that sense of wasted time and a sense that you inflicted hurt upon others. Well, love believes the best—*even about yourself.*

This verse in The Amplified Bible says even more. "Love bears up under anything and everything that comes, is **ever ready to believe the best of every person**" (1 Corinthians 13:7). Since you are an "every person," you may need to *actively forgive yourself.*

"Well, I don't feel forgiven," you say. Good! We wouldn't want you to simply respond to your feelings; feelings are fickle. God is not a feeling or an emotion. *God is a spirit*—a life-giving Sprit who will change your feelings and emotions. *The real you is your spirit man.* In fact, you are a spirit, you live in a body, and you possess a mind (will and emotions).

So act like you are forgiven, because guess what, you are forgiven! Act like you are forgiven and those feelings of true righteousness, holiness and forgiveness will follow. Believe the best about yourself. God is the Redeemer, and He is redeeming your whole life from destruction. The same blood that redeemed you and changed your entire life also is flowing to your family and friends. It's flowing toward your job. Its boundless waves crash forward to make a way for your future. Then the tide goes out and His blood washes backward—back to your past to redeem it.

Believe on the Lord Jesus Christ, and you and your household will be saved. He is the Alpha and Omega—your beginning and your end. And He is your righteousness. So believe the best about yourself, forgive yourself, and watch Him make all things new.

Look at all this preaching and exhortation that has flowed about *forgiving yourself.* This is what happens when we *follow the inward witness and allow the Holy Spirit to highlight, accentuate and bear witness to scriptures.* Not only do blessed scriptures come alive and brand us, but also whole paragraphs of thought, new volumes of blessed thinking and mind-sets of goodness begin to develop. They preach to us, transform us, encourage us, heal us and conform us to His blessed and merciful attitudes and intents for us.

Through these orations of unction or anointing, we are convinced of God's love and plans for us. Our Bibles begin to preach to us—speak to us—as He who was thought dead proves to us again and again that He is alive and well! Oh, my friend, this is Bible study and true fellowship with the Godhead.

CHAPTER 10

MORE AWESOME EXAMPLES OF FOLLOWING THE **INWARD WITNESS**

This Includes the Story of a 'Velveeta-like' Substance Coming out of My Nose

(Yes, this is another section subhead because, as you can see, there are capital letters for each word. Then again, it is very long and normally would not be thought of as a section heading, but I am writing this book and these are my versions of section headings.)

When I first went to Bible school, I took a job waiting tables and left my purchasing position with a marketing firm. I left a job that offered benefits, a future, steady paychecks and paid vacations to pursue God's call and study the Bible.

For sure I wasn't making a lot of money waiting tables, which meant it wasn't good news that every two or three months I'd get a sinus infection. Oh yeah. While in my first year at Bible school, I was visited with a quarterly sinus infection. I had endured them for years, and they weren't a big deal before when I had insurance benefits to pay the doctor's bills. But a waitress job with no benefits meant that going to the doctor was a tremendously big deal.

I will stop right here and qualify myself. I believe staunchly in going to the doctor. No matter what you have heard preachers or crazy Christians say, doctors are wonderful and absolutely necessary. Christians who do not believe in going to doctors are moving in doubt, unbelief and presumption. Go to the doctor! I have the most awesome doctor ever. He is amazing. If I were not convinced that healing was provided for me in the Lord, I would be praying to get sick because my doctor is that amazing! So go to the doctor, and never say I told you not to go.

Anyway, back to the sinus infection. Not only did I not have any health benefits to cover a doctor's   visit and prescriptions, but also the infections I'd been experiencing required the ever-increasing power of antibiotic. My immune system had built up a resistance, and the antibiotics needed were becoming more and more expensive. Also, it seemed we were quickly approaching the end of my antibiotic options because I was reaching the top of the line as it were.

Help!

I decided I needed to go to the Word of God regarding the subject of healing. It's always important to go to the Word of God regarding a subject that concerns you and to pray *the Ephesians prayer regarding the subject about which you need revelation.* Then open your Bible to the New Testament and see which scriptures begin to jump out at you.

You may also want to purchase a Strong's Exhaustive Concordance of the Bible. You can get one at any Bible bookstore. It's a book that lists individual words in the Bible. Let's say you wanted to see which scriptures included the word *light*. Well, you would open your concordance, and look up the word *light*. Viol`a! A complete list of scriptures containing the word *light* will unfold before you.

So in the situation regarding the sinus infection, I opened my concordance and looked up any words I could think of in connection with *healing*. I looked up *healed, heal, healing, health, sick, sickness*. Quite frankly, I even looked up *nose, breath, breathe, fever* and *infection*. I prayed the Ephesians prayer over myself, and then I headed to my Bible to look up those scriptures.

Of all the scriptures I looked up, the following passages jumped out at me and were highlighted to me by the Holy Spirit. He seemed to seize upon or bear witness to them so I wrote them down. I also wrote down what I felt the Holy Spirit was saying to me **about** them.

Luke 23:46-47 speaks of Jesus on the Cross. Verse 46 says, " … When Jesus had cried out with a loud voice, He said, 'Father, into Your hands I commit My spirit.' Having said this, He *breathed* His last." Jesus paid the price for our salvation on the Cross. In the literal Hebrew, Isaiah 53:5 tells us that Jesus was wounded for our sickness and carried away our pain. Whatever Jesus bore on the Cross, He bore so you and I don't have to bear it now. He bore all things spiritually, mentally and physically as He then *breathed* His last.

That scripture, and particularly, that word *breathed* jumped out at me and were highlighted by the Holy Spirit. So I wrote down the scripture and dared to believe 1 John 2:27—that the anointing would teach *me*. I wrote down what I felt the Holy Spirit was saying to me or teaching me *about* that scripture. Woo hoo! *By allowing the Holy Spirit to teach me, I was letting the Word abide in me.*

So, in my journal or notebook, I wrote the following: Luke 23:46-47, " ... When Jesus had cried out with a loud voice, He said, 'Father, into your hands I commit My spirit.' Having said this, He **breathed** His last." I usually underline, but you can highlight, pile on smiley faces or add whatever other notations, cartoons or illustrations that will greatly emphasize how you're acknowledging the importance of certain words in scripture.

Then I wrote whatever thoughts started coming to me regarding these scriptures. At first they may seem as familiar to me as my own thoughts. But the more I write, the more these mortal thoughts become inspired, and the Holy Spirit is *released* to convince me of how healed I am. He takes hold together with me against fear, doubt, unbelief—and the very infirmity itself.

With the pen of a ready writer, I wrote the following words: "The last thing Jesus did was to give up His own breath. If He sacrificed His breath for me, then He paid the price for me to be able to breathe and to breathe clear and free and with ease." Then I looked at what I just wrote and something stood out to me in that. The word *last* stood out to me. Suddenly from on the inside I remembered or began to wonder, *Didn't God breathe the breath of life into Adam in the book of Genesis? Hmmm, I wonder if that's true? I wonder if that's right? I wonder if that's just me making it up?* So, I went back to my concordance and once again looked up the words *breath, breathe* and *breathed.* Oh, my goodness, there it was! The word *breathed* is in the book of Genesis.

Wow! The concordance said it was in Genesis 2:6-7 so I turned right over there and excitedly read, "And the Lord God formed man of the dust of the ground, and breathed into his nostrils the breath of life; and man became a living being." Wow! I was amazed! The Holy Spirit was actually putting me in remembrance of what the Word says. He was on the job convincing me of my blessing. He was breaking open the Word in such a way that *the faith of God* was stirred and increased in my heart.

Excitedly I wrote down that scripture, and then I wrote down what the Holy Spirit seemed to be saying to me about that scripture. In other words, I wrote down what thoughts or encouragement seemed to be coming to me. I wrote down why I was feeling blessed about this scripture. My heart was astounding my mind.

I wrote: "Breathing life into Adam was the *first* thing God did to Adam. When Jesus arose from the dead and appeared to the disciples, He breathed upon them and told them to receive the Holy Spirit. Thus, men were born again for the first time! (John 20:22). Breathing was the *first thing* God did to Adam, and *it made Him alive, quickened Him as it were.* If breathing was the first thing God did to Adam and the first thing Jesus did to the disciples, then breathing must be a priority to God. Also, if Adam was quickened or made alive by the breath of God, and Jesus quickened or made alive the disciples with His breath—then, *with every breath I take my sinuses are made alive and quickened!*

"Oh yeah! It looks like breathing is pretty important to God. It's the first thing He did! Therefore, God is concerned about my breathing. If Jesus paid the price for me to breathe easy and it was such a priority that it was the first thing God did with Adam, then I believe I can breathe freely, easily and with no infection. I believe I am healed. I believe I am free of a sinus infection. I believe the same quickening and encouragement being ministered to me by the Holy Spirit is quickening and making alive my mortal body. Therefore, I am healed!"

I continued to look up scriptures and came across Mark 5:25-34. I read of a woman who had been hemorrhaging for 12 years. She had spent all the money she had on physicians, but could not be healed by any. Then one day she came up from behind and touched the border of Jesus' garment, and immediately she was healed.

This scripture in the Gospels absolutely jumped out at me. I wrote it down, and I also wrote down the following: "This woman received healing from the Lord even *before* His death, burial and resurrection. I live *after* the death, burial and resurrection of Jesus, and thus I live under a *better covenant*. How much more does healing belong to me? Also, I was reminded of the scripture in 1 John 4:4, "...Greater is He that is in you, than he that is in the world!" Jesus lives in me! That woman touched Jesus as He walked past her, yet I have Jesus living on the *inside of me!* I am in touch with His power all the time! Greater is He that is in me than sickness or disease that would try to stay in me!"

At that point I threw my pen down as I sensed the quickening, witnessing, attesting and overwhelming power of the Lord rise up inside me and begin to confirm. I couldn't stay seated any longer. I jumped up and began to shout the scripture and shout what the Holy Ghost prompted me to say. It is like I no longer liveth, but truly Christ is living His life through me. I jumped! I shouted! I rejoiced in the Lord—and suddenly—*POP!* My sinuses opened! And over the next two days every one of my symptoms left! Woo hoo!

We talk about how the Holy Spirit will bear witness to the Word. But get this: God wants you to **be a witness** to His power and experience it firsthand. The Holy Ghost will quicken, highlight and bear witness to scriptures. Then, as you write them down and meditate on them and even dare to speak those scriptures, *the power of the Lord that's present to heal will begin to well up on the inside of you!* You will experience and **be a witness** to His exceedingly great healing power!

I FOUND MYSELF IN THE BOOK OF ACTS

When we pray the prayer found in Ephesians 1:17-23, it's an act of faith that sets our heart to receive from the Word of God. If we will pray this prayer and then expose ourselves to God's Word, God will speak to us by the witness of His Spirit. His Words will be illuminated to us whether we're reading His words in the Bible, in a book or listening to a preacher, pastor or teacher speak them.

When I was in Bible school, I would pray every morning for myself and for the preachers and teachers who would be teaching me that day. I would pray the Ephesians prayer over myself, and I would pray an additional prayer found in Ephesians 6:19-20 over the instructors, preachers and teachers who would minister that day.

The apostle Paul also wrote this additional prayer and instructed the saints of his day to pray it for him. The fact that Paul would ask others for prayer totally captivated my attention. I mean, this is Paul the apostle we're talking about who wrote a huge portion of the New Testament and whose revelations we are still believing to unravel. He was a man of such love that he wished himself accursed so his brethren might be saved. Yet, amazingly enough, this is the same Paul who said he needed the saints to pray for Him in order that he make known the gospel as he ought.

Well now, think about this. If Paul needed the saints to pray for *him* so he could make revelation known to them, then don't you suppose *we* need to pray for our ministers so they can make the gospel known to us? Don't you suppose we should pray for our ministers as an act of help so our hearts can and will pull on that gifting in them? Absolutely! Praying for ministers sets your heart in an attitude of expectancy so you can really get what the Lord has for you through a minister. Paul knew that if the saints would pray for him, he would be enabled and empowered by God to speak to them. Therefore, we should pray this prayer for ministers who stand before us to speak.

So, again, I prayed Ephesians 6:19-20 every day for my instructors so utterance would be given unto (my instructors),that (they) would open (their) mouths boldly to make known the mystery of the gospel, for which (they were) ambassadors in chains; that in it (they) would speak boldly, as (they) ought to speak. As a result when I walked through a classroom door, I fully expected God to speak to me through my instructors.

And I expected even more than that! I expected the Holy Spirit to personalize the lesson for me. As the instructors would teach, I would write down the information they were sharing. But then, just like when I read my Bible during private study, something they said would captivate my attention and explode on the inside of me. Something they would share—a scripture, a revelation, an example, a phrase, a quote, maybe even a gesture—would cause my heart to bear witness to what was said. So I would write down those thoughts just as I did in my private study time, knowing full well that my faith had opened the door for the Holy Spirit to expound on what was taught.

You see, the prayer I had prayed in Ephesians 1:17-23 was supplying me with revelation, wisdom and knowledge. The prayer I had prayed in Ephesians 6:19-20 was also at work and supplying me with supernatural utterance from my instructors. I was receiving these teachers in faith, and the prayers I had prayed allowed me to exercise faith toward God that *He* would speak to me.

Let me challenge you to pray these prayers for your pastor before you go to church on Sunday morning. See what a marvelous change there will be in your pastor's preaching! Actually, you'll probably end up wondering, *Did my pastor really change? Or, did I just start getting scriptural in my prayers? Did my pastor suddenly become the oracle of God, or am I finally listening with my heart?* Both these Ephesians prayers allowed me to exercise faith toward God that His pastors, ministers and instructors would speak to me. And speak to me, He always did.

At school I was drawn to one instructor in particular who taught on many things. However, there was a certain phrase he'd use every now and then that my "spirit man" would quicken to me. When the instructor would speak a certain phrase it would leap out at me like flashes of lightning in the night sky. I'm telling you, when he'd speak that particular phrase it would charge me, provoke me and draw me to it. The phrase would brand my heart.

My head may have been distracted and my body may have been tired that day, but because I had prayed those prayers my spirit was revved up and ready in faith. My "spirit man" would rise up on the inside of me and grasp and apprehend the phrase each time it was uttered. My spirit—infused, inhabited and influenced by the Holy Spirit—knew that phrase had something to do with the plan of God for my life.

The phrase I am speaking of that so impacted me is "*the Word and the Spirit.*" The instructor I described would often emphasize that Christians must have the *written* Word, but yet yield to the *Spirit* of God. In fact, that is the premise of this book. The book you are reading right now is about the importance of reading the *written Word* of God and allowing the *Spirit of God* to speak to you first and foremost through the Word. If you have these two mighty forces—the written Word of God and the Spirit of God—working together through you *then* you will hear the voice of God, and you will find and do the will of God.

Later I was reading Acts 6 and 7 as I had done many times before, yet something was different. These passages had never before spoken to me as they did on that day. As I finished reading Chapters 1 through 5 and began Chapters 6 and 7, my heart began to "heat up" and certain phrases began to attract me. I "camped" right there for a while.

The passages deal with a man named Stephen who was a church member. In those days the church was growing so fast that the disciples found themselves in need of help. They wanted to give themselves further to study God's Word and to prayer so they would be better equipped to help the growing congregation. So they looked for individuals to help them with the work load of waiting on tables and physically helping the growing masses with the natural labors associated with a church. For instance, the Bible says they needed help distributing food to widows as well as many other tasks.

Even though there were many people to choose from, only seven were to be selected for this precious activity of service in the Lord's house. They had to be people of a high caliber of integrity. Isn't that awesome? A person may only be sweeping church floors, but brother if God is having the person do that, he or she must have a wonderful heart and be full of integrity and full of faith. Thank God for workers in the church today who have a heart just like that.

As I continued reading the qualifications for these divine waiters, something began to jump out at me. Acts 6:3-4 says, "Therefore, brethren, seek out from among you seven men of good reputation, full of the Holy Spirit and wisdom, whom we may appoint over this business...."

As soon as I read that phrase, *"full of the Holy Spirit and wisdom,"* the Holy Ghost instantly quickened it to me. He reminded me of what that instructor had said about the importance of *the Word and the Spirit.* You see, people who allow the Holy Spirit to bear witness to the scriptures are people who get full of the power and presence of the Spirit. People who allow the Holy Spirit to teach them the scriptures are literally "being filled with the Spirit as He is speaking."

Then, in that same instant, the Holy Spirit reminded me that *wisdom* is always in connection with the Word of God. Wisdom is what the Holy Spirit can produce if the *written* Word of God is stockpiled and then "broken open" in our hearts. After all, wisdom comes from the Word of God via the Holy Spirit. Therefore, in this scripture, I saw that divine recipe of *the Word and the Spirit* once again. WOW!

That means these first individuals selected by the Holy Ghost to serve in the early church were people of *the Word and the Spirit.* I then reasoned that people God would use today or any other day would also be people of the Word and the Spirit. People the Holy Spirit hand selects—people who will be separated out and promoted by divine decree—will be Christians who read God's Word and allow the Spirit to teach, train and prepare them. WOW again! So I wrote all that down. I wrote down the scripture and what I believed the Holy Spirit had revealed to me about that scripture.

I continued reading Acts 6:5, which says, "And they chose Stephen, a man full of *faith* and the *Holy Spirit,* and Philip, Prochorus, Nicanor, Timon, Parmenas, and Nicolas, a proselyte from Antioch...." Even though this scripture lists all these men, the passage only goes on to expound upon one man—namely Stephen.

Acts 6:8 says, "Stephen, *full of faith and power,*
did great wonders and signs among the people." In
the midst of describing Stephen, my heart was again
quickened. My heart began to prompt me, remind
me and instruct me; it was not an audible voice, but
a "downloading" of insight. All of the sudden, I just
kind of knew or was reminded that Romans 10:17
says, "Faith comes by hearing and hearing by the
Word of God." Now notice this: Faith comes from the
Word of God. So there's the *Word,* and Stephen was
definitely a man of the Word. Then I was reminded of
Mark 16:20, which says the job of the Holy Spirit is to
"*confirm the Word with signs, wonders and miracles.*"
That's the power and demonstration of the Holy
Spirit, and that's the Spirit of God at work.

Then I realized Stephen was a man of the Word
and the Spirit. *This Bible passage in Acts 6 had
become as a living, breathing "teacher" to me.* It
seemed as though Acts 6 had become alive and
was standing up like my teachers in school at the
head of the classroom, pointer in hand, teaching me
about Stephen. *Acts 6 was teaching me about the
qualifications to be used by God and illustrating
to me how to find the will of God.* Acts 6 was
introducing me to Stephen, and ultimately, Acts 6
*would introduce me—**to me!***

I continued to read. The Holy Spirit again caused
my eyes to be riveted by Acts 6:10. Like popcorn
popping, this scripture leaped out at me. Acts 6:10
says of Stephen and the people to whom he spoke,
"*they [the people] were not able to resist the **wisdom**
and the **Spirit** by which he [Stephen] spoke.*"

Whoa—there it is again! The scriptures were emphasizing to me that Stephen was a man of *the Word and the Spirit!* Does anyone else see this? Hello McFly—is anybody home? I mean, it's as though I was driving down a highway and giant Holy Spirit billboards were shouting out to me.

The passage had developed a flow. It was as though this text had ceased to be a book full of print. An easy conversation had developed, and the Bible would speak and my heart would acknowledge and answer in agreement. This activity seemed to bypass my mental capacities and their abilities to interrupt.

At some point I couldn't even tell the difference between the Bible and me. No longer just agreement, the pages had grabbed me and integrated me into the scenario I was reading. I saw myself as Stephen. As I continued to read, certain actions, words and attitudes of Stephen described in the passage became *me* doing and saying things. What I was reading became like a movie, and I was in it. I continued to watch in expectation to see what Stephen would do and what I—Stephen— would become.

Acts 6:15 says of Stephen, " ...and all who sat in the council, looking steadfastly at him, saw his face as the face of an angel." Whatever Stephen was doing caused a supernatural manifestation of the power of God. Either the people listening to him were granted a vision of an angel or his skin started glowing and shining with the glory of God. I believe the latter. As I read this scripture, I was reminded of 1 Corinthians 15:51-53 that speaks of the saints of God suddenly changed by the glory of God. I was reminded of how the corruptibility in our human flesh will be swallowed up, transfigured and transformed into a glorified body fit to fly through the portal of the rapture.

I felt quickened by the Holy Spirit that part of my own ministry would reflect this aspect I saw in Stephen. I began to see that if a preacher would preach the power of *the Word and the Spirit,* somehow it would catalyze or propel the saints into the place of transformation and help to trip the trigger of the rapture of the church.

You might wonder, *How in the world did you get all that?* I just prayed the Ephesians prayer, read my scriptures and dared to let the Holy Ghost speak to me. My friend, He will speak to you as well if you will let Him.

He will speak amazing things to you.

He will reveal the Lord to you.

He will reveal *you* to *you.*

People worship and magnify the Lord when they see miracles of healing. People bow and magnify God as sick people get out of wheelchairs; I have seen it. However, there are also amazing displays of the wisdom of God—manifestations of awe-inspiring revelations as could only emanate from the Spirit of God. These demonstrations of the eternal wisdom of God are what speak to me and change me. They instill an instant humility.

They show me the greatness of the Godhead and how dependent I am upon Him. I thank God for these manifestations. It brings great peace and trust to my heart for He is greater than I, wiser than I. I rest in such sovereign vastness. These manifestations of revelation are what transform the saint and conform him or her to the plan and purpose of God. These manifestations are the mirror by which a saint can see who he or she really is and then ultimately become that image.

The finale of all these thoughts came to me as I continued reading in Acts 7:55-56. The verses tells us, "But he [Stephen], being full of the Holy Spirit, gazed into heaven and saw the glory of God, and Jesus standing at the right hand of God, and said, Look! I see the heavens opened and the Son of Man standing at the right hand of God!"

As I read these final verses, the Lord quickened to me, "If you will be a preacher of *the Word and of the Spirit*, this will not only help to catalyze the change of the saints from mortal to immortality, but also you along with other preachers and believers everywhere will cause an opening in the heavens."

Think about it. Stephen's actions, life and preaching catalyzed some kind of portal of the glory, and he saw Jesus *standing* at that opening. Ephesians 1:20 tells us that after Jesus' death, burial and resurrection, He was *seated* at the right hand of the Father. According to the context of scripture, Jesus *was seated*. Yet, according to Stephen, Jesus *was standing*. Whoa! In other words, something Stephen did caused the Lord to *stand up* at a portal of glory. For that matter, something Stephen did catalyzed "the heavens to open." Something Stephen did caused the heavens to open in such a way that He and Jesus were looking at each other—ready to meet!

It was as if Jesus Himself was showing us how to finish things up, ***how to cause the harvest of the earth***

to respond to the gospel. And thus, we were shown how to catalyze the Lord Jesus Himself from a place of sitting to a place of **standing** to go collect and welcome His Church home. The Lord went on to speak to my heart and said, "If you will be a preacher of *the Word and the Spirit*, the lost and the saints will respond. They will be changed and won into the kingdom. You and others will help to cause an opening in the atmosphere of this age, and Jesus will arise and come for His Church."

It was as though through the revelation of the Spirit of God, Stephen had become a living example of how to open a powerful door, a door so powerful even Jesus Himself would say, "Wow, I see preachers finally moving with both *the Word and the Spirit*. I see the saints putting the Word of God first and yielding in prayer to the power of the Holy Spirit. I see the saints starting to glow under the Spirit's power and becoming a sign and wonder to the lost. Beginning to arise, Jesus asks, *"Father, is it time for me to go now? Can I go now to get my Church?"* It sure looks like a foretaste, if not the actual display of the glory that is to come. Hallelujah!

YOU ARE IN THE BIBLE

No doubt, your heart *bears witness* to these truths. As you've been reading about the Word and the Spirit, it's as though the page grabs you and pulls you in. Your heart begins to burn with the fire of this truth, and you are emboldened and inspired to serve God even more. You are challenged to find *yourself* within His great plan and purpose.

You know that *you* also can be found somewhere

within the pages of your Bible.

Let's help you find *you* by reading about two men who encountered the Lord Jesus after His death, burial and resurrection. Luke 24 says the two men did not recognize Jesus by face for His physical appearance was altered. He was no longer flesh and blood, but was flesh and bone because He was glorified and transfigured. Yet even though these men did not recognize Jesus in the natural, they describe how they came to know and realize that it was actually the Lord who had spoken with them.

Luke 24:31-33 says, "Then their eyes were opened and they knew Him; and He vanished from their sight. And they said to one another, 'Did not **our hearts burn within us** while He talked with us on the road, and while **He opened the scriptures to us?'** " This is a perfect description of how we are to know our Savior through the Word. **We know Him after the Spirit.** The Bible says we do not know any man after the flesh, not even Jesus Christ.

My friend, when you read scriptures or books inspired by the Holy Spirit, your heart will begin to burn within you **bearing witness** to His words, His voice and His power. Your heart will begin **to burn** and **bear witness** to scripture, teaching and ministries that are a part of the plan of God for your life. Your heart will **bear witness** to correct decisions. Your heart will **bear witness** with leadings, promptings, answers, direction, revelation and guidance that will come directly from the Lord. And the action of your heart as the Holy Spirit **bears witness will make you into a witness.**

In Luke 4:16-18, Jesus was preaching from the book of Isaiah in the Old Testament. He quoted

Isaiah 61:1-2 that says, "The Spirit of the Lord God is upon Me, because He has anointed Me to preach good tidings [the gospel] to the poor; He has sent Me to heal the broken hearted, to proclaim liberty to the captives, and the opening of the prison to those who are bound; to proclaim the acceptable year of the Lord." After quoting from the Old Testament, Jesus told the people, "Today this scripture is fulfilled in your hearing" (Luke 4:21). You see Jesus walked the earth as a man anointed by the Holy Ghost, but He also came to give us an example of how we should walk in the earth. The blessed truth conveyed in this book, You Can Pray, is perfectly illustrated in this passage of Luke.

There's no doubt that as Jesus was reading the book of Isaiah one day, His eyes fell upon the first few verses of Isaiah 61, and His heart bore witness that the very scripture He was reading was a portrait of Him and His calling. Jesus **found Himself** in the Word of God. As He recognized and acknowledged that inner witness, He then **became** that scripture. Literally—the Word was made flesh.

We are not above our Master. Jesus is the example of following the will of God. And just like Jesus, dear one, **you** are somewhere in the scriptures! As you search the scriptures, you will recognize and acknowledge who **you** are. You will follow the inward witness. As you find yourself in a passage, you will then stand like Jesus and say, "Today is this scripture fulfilled in your hearing!" Imagine that. You are in the Bible!

People will begin to watch your life and see that you walk in favor, blessings, healing, prosperity, joy and peace as though led by some great unseen guidance. By following the *"Bear Witness-er,"* people will see that trials do not affect you in the same way. They will see that through following the *"Bear Witness-er,"* events and happenings turn out for good in your life. By following the *witness of the Spirit* people will watch *you,* and you will become a *witness* of how the Lord is working in your life. Others who do not know God will become a *witness* of Him through you! Through your acknowledgment of the scriptures and audacity to respond to Him—the lost will have an opportunity to see God.

As you follow that *witness,* you will be led into the blessings of God for your family, job, business or career. As you follow that *witness,* He can and will lead you off of the bed of sickness. As you follow that *witness,* you will be led into the supreme calling of your life—whatever that may be—and you will be a *witness for Him.* Hallelujah!

CHAPTER 11

THE SPIRIT HAS LED YOU **THROUGH** THE BIBLE, NOW HE **CAN** LEAD YOU IN PRAYER

Rewards and benefits are ready to unfold before your eyes—or better yet, in your prayers. Let's take a look at your track record and what you've accomplished so we'll understand exactly what's going to unfold for you.

We've talked about how the first step to effectual prayer is continual study of God's Word and how important it is to pray the Ephesians prayer. We've talked about how important it is to open your Bible to the New Testament and let scriptures jump out and be quickened to you. And we've talked about how you should follow this blueprint for prayer every time you read your Bible so the Word of God can continually teach you.

As you've been faithful to apply these principles and adopt this lifestyle of prayer, you've approached the Word by faith, ever ready to hear. Therefore, in accordance with 1 John 2:27, you've allowed the anointing of the Holy Spirit to teach you, so shall His words *abide* in you. And you've been ever aware that John 15:7-8 says if His words **abide** in you, you will ask or go in to the realm of prayer, and it shall be done for you.

So, friend, you've done well! You've studied to show yourself approved unto God, a workman who needs not be ashamed, rightly dividing the Word of Truth. You have allowed the Holy Ghost to first and foremost **lead and guide you into the truth of God's Word**.

In other words, you've been a "doer" of the scripture found in John 16:13. The first part of the verse says, "He will lead and guide you into **all** the truth .... " But hold on! Because you've satisfied the **condition** stated in the first part of John 16:13, now you're in a prime position to claim the second half of the verse. Take a look right here at your promised reward.

John 16:13

"However, when He, the Spirit of Truth has come, **He will guide you into all truth**; for He will not speak on His own authority, but whatever He hears He will speak, and **He will tell you things to come**."

Wow! "The Spirit of Truth," as the scripture calls Him will guide you into all the truth. No wonder— Psalm 119:160 says of God, "Thy Word is Truth, O Lord." What else does John 16:13 promise? It promises that the Spirit of Truth will tell you what He hears, and He will tell you things to come. Woo hoo! Now there's something to shout about! He will show you events, peoples and nations. He will reveal God's plans for **you!**

EVER READY TO PRAY

Yet, there's more! As you've followed the Spirit of Truth through the truth of God's Word and allowed yourself to be trained as He's quickened and highlighted words and phrases to you, something else very important has happened. *You've become familiar with His voice, His witness and His leading.* So He who has led you **through the Word** now will lead you **in prayer** and show you *things to come that are not written down in scriptures.*

Now, my friend, **you are ready to pray!**

My, my, my, but you are ready to pray, and the "Bear Witness-er" of the Holy Ghost is also ever ready to pray. My, my, my but the adventures and wondrous times you are about to experience. You will be amazed at the compassion that flows from your belly toward situations and people. You will be amazed at the "knowings" you will have regarding situations and events. Revelations will flow sweet. You will sense the Greater One, and you will *work with Him.* You will help make a way for the calling of Jesus on the earth; you will come to know Him by experience. You will be changed, and you will do the will of God, becoming an answer even to many of the prayers the Spirit of God will inspire you to pray.

Because you have trained your heart to follow the witness of the Holy Spirit in the staunch written Word, your heart has become a safe guide to follow that same witness through life's events and into the plan of God for your life.

Follow the simple format in the place of prayer.

Pray the Ephesians prayer over yourself at the beginning of your prayer time—pray it and mean it. Then as you think of people or places, names, nations and situations, take a risk. That's right—*go out on a limb, and dare to pray in your understanding about these promptings. You see, when you pray the Ephesians prayer at the beginning of your prayer time, you are authorizing the Holy Spirit to lead you.* This very prayer prayed at the onset of your prayer time will actually **cause** these perceptions, thoughts and promptings to arise in your heart.

Dare to follow the witness of the Spirit to lead you in specifics not written down. Dare to follow the promptings, thoughts, pictures, events and peoples that the witness of the Spirit brings to you. Dare to follow the compassions, joy, mercies, impressions, boldness and holiest of emotions He would stir in you—that person's face from church, that story on the news, our president, children in Somalia, that missionary, your pastor, your husband, your child, that person who made you mad. Yes, that's right! Follow those impressions that the *"Bear Witness-er"* bears witness to in your prayer time.

Of course, as we've discussed the most simple and effectual format for prayer is to first pray the Ephesians prayer at the beginning of your Bible study time. Let scriptures jump out at you, write them down and follow that *witness* through the Word. *Then, when you enter your prayer time, pray the Ephesians prayer again at the beginning,* and *pray in your understanding as far as you know to pray.* But don't stop there! **Take a risk and pray about things that come up on the inside of you.**

The Spirit of Truth can help you get down to the

nitty-gritty in prayer—the very specifics of your life and purpose. For instance, suppose you don't see your name written in the Bible. Does that mean God does not have a plan for you? Of course not.

Stick with me here. I have ministered in a town called Flippin, Arkansas. Believe me, the word *Flippin* is sooo not in the Bible. So does that mean that God does not have a plan for Flippin, Arkansas? Does it also mean it was not the will of God for me to go to Flippin? No way. God has a plan for Flippin, Arkansas, like God has a plan for you.

Names aren't the end-all here. In fact, there are all kinds of strange names in the Bible. There is a man in the Bible who had two daughters, *Athaliah* and *Hoglah*. Dear me, shouldn't it be a sin to name someone that? On the other hand, the name *Deborah* is in the Bible, but that doesn't mean God's will or plan for every *Deborah* is outlined in chapter and verse. Wouldn't that be interesting? Calling all *Deborahs!* Turn to Acts 14 to find your plan. No, it doesn't work that way.

But here's how it does work. The same *witness* that led me through the scriptures during my Bible study is the same *witness* of the Spirit who prompted me to go to Flippin, Arkansas. He's the same Witness who has a plan for you whether your name is Deborah or Athaliah or Hoglah—or even if your name is not found in the Bible at all. Again, the same *witness* that lead you and me through God's Word is the same *witness* who will lead you and me in prayer.

Think of it this way. God's Word—or truth—is like a spiritual *railroad track* that your prayers must run on or travel on. You need track laid out so your train engine has a course to navigate. News flash: No track—no effectual prayer. If there is no track, then the saint is headed for derailment, havoc and even though it sounds corny—a *train wreck*.

In prayer you are traveling out into the spirit realm, and so it's important to travel in spirit and in truth. John 4:24 tells us, "God is Spirit, and those who worship Him must worship in spirit and truth." Indeed, going out into the spirit realm, worshipping God in spirit and truth, protects you. After all, in the realm of the spirit, there are many spirits, many voices and none without signification. There are demon spirits and familiar spirits, and there is even the influence of your emotions and thought processes. But, thank God, there's also a *Holy* Spirit who has trained you in the Word and now leads you **in the spirit**.

SUPERNATURAL HELP THROUGH THE WORD

God has given us the most supernatural help possible—He's put His own Spirit on the inside of every born-again believer. It's a miracle! The creator of the universe is willing to deposit His very own Spirit on the inside of you and me *to help us* through the Word, in prayer and in life.

No wonder the Spirit of God is called "the Helper" in John 14:26 because He truly *helps us* in our daily lives and in the area of prayer. He is also likened unto the *glory* of God or the *anointing* of God. Romans 6:4 says, " ... *just as Christ was raised from the dead by the glory of the Father, even so we also should walk in newness of life.*"

The Bible also calls Him the "Spirit of Truth" in John

14:17. Inspired by the Spirit of Truth, men of old wrote the Bible. Men of old yielded to the Holy Spirit to write the Old Testament and men of not quite so old yielded to the Holy Spirit to write the New Testament. How do we know? Because as born-again Christians we read both the Old Testament and the New Testament, and the Holy Spirit begins to show us how they connect.

He will take a scripture in the New Testament and without any effort on our part connect it to an example or picture in the Old Testament that illustrates a New Testament truth. We begin to see that although the words may be different from the Old Testament to the New Testament—maybe even the attitude or actions differ from one to the other—yet somehow, the **spirit of both testaments agrees**.

How can that be? Well, my friend, the proof is in the pudding or in the eating. I challenge you to ask Jesus into your heart. (Check out Chapter 17 right now to make that commitment!) Then I also challenge you to pray the Ephesians prayer and begin reading God's Word. Let the Spirit that wrote the scriptures through men of old prove God's Word to you. It's a miracle, my friend. It's an ongoing miracle.

The Holy Spirit will show us truths and revelations in the New Testament and then lead us into the Old Testament for pictures, types, shadows and illustrations of New Testament truths. We will see that the spirit of the Old Testament and the New Testament agree. We will see that the spirit of the context agrees.

In fact, this is how the books of the Bible were chosen; certain ones had the "same spirit" about them. The spirit of the books, though written by different individuals and at times thousands of years apart, was still the same because of *the Spirit—the Holy Spirit who authored them.* The same Spirit was obviously leading and guiding these individuals. It is uncanny and so amazingly supernatural how the spirit of these books agrees.

Consider this. Say you receive a letter from your mom. Then say you receive another letter from someone playing a joke on you, and he or she fills the letter with terrible news to frighten you. Perhaps the person ends up signing your mother's name or even forging her handwriting.

You read it and think, *Hmmm—same handwriting. Wow, my mom even uses that phrase a lot, but still, there is something funny here. I don't know what it is, but this letter just does not sound like my mom.* "There's just something about the letter I don't buy. I really should believe it. I mean, her signature is there," you explain, talking to a friend. "But, well, I just know my mom and something about this is not my mom at all." You wonder if it's a hoax or a joke because something is amiss, something is just not right. *I just know—I don't know how—but I know this is not my mom,* you conclude.

That same process is how spiritual leaders knew to put the letters or books of the Bible together. Even though terminology might have been close and stories may have been fascinating, if it was not the **same spirit,** they threw it out or did not allow it as the "Canon" of scripture. Though amazing, titillating and even true, if it did not have the *same spirit* about it, they did not allow it.

They couldn't afford to; scripture is too important.

Scripture is what we call doctrine, and doctrine is the pathway of your spiritual life. So if you don't have the right path, then you don't have the right leading into the spirit realm—it's not the right spirit leading.

Thus, the scriptures agree because they are of the same spirit. That is why we pray the Ephesians prayer, study our Bible and let the Holy Spirit speak and teach the scriptures to us because ...

The scriptures carry the same Spirit

we are wanting to follow

into the spirit realm when we pray!

HOLY GHOST HELP IN PRAYER

The same Spirit who has led us through our Bibles and taught us, is the same Spirit who will lead us into the spirit realm via the avenue of prayer. With all the experience of God's Word supporting us as a vital foundation of truth and accuracy, He even will be able to show and tell us personal things and events to come not specifically written in the Word of God.

As we will allow the Holy Spirit free course throughout the Word of God—connecting scriptures, highlighting passages, familiarizing us with the fabric, feel, sound, flavor and sense of the very spirit of the written Word—then that same Spirit can lead and guide us in prayer. He will be able to successfully reveal and show us people, nations, events, places and blessings that will be pertinent to the plans and purposes of God in the earth and our personal lives.

Remember: Pray the Ephesians prayer over yourself

at the beginning of your prayer time. Pray it and mean it. Pray the whole prayer. Then step out in your understanding and begin to pray around the leadings prompted in your heart. As you do this, you may start out a little wobbly regarding these "divine ideas," but as you follow the Holy Spirit, He will take hold with you. Soon you'll begin to pray wonderful, divine utterances by inspiration. You will sense His quickening, His thoughts, His empowerment. Woo hoo! It's fun. Your eyes will try to look down and see the amazing things your mouth is doing because the Holy Spirit has begun to *help* you pray. Remember—He is *your Helper*.

For instance, a person's name may rise up on the inside. You may be suddenly conscious of a leader, a city, a nation. You may have a dream that causes you to wake up and suddenly enter into prayer, rebuking the havoc and devastation you saw in your sleep. You may suddenly find yourself thinking about a change in your job situation. You may wonder, *Is that just me thinking that? Am I just making that up? What should I do with that? Brush it off and ignore it?*

As you become familiar with following the Spirit of Truth through the truth of God's Word, *then when certain sensations, warnings, feelings or even visions come to you that are of significance to God's will,* **they will have the same feel or same spirit about them you sensed when you read your Bible.** *Think about what this can mean to you and how it can help you. These sensations, warnings, feelings or visions will be* **God speaking to you, and you can effectively take them back into prayer.**

If they are sensations of warning and havoc, you will take authority over them in the name of Jesus, speaking life, protection and blessing into those situations. If they are premonitions of change or blessing, you pray the Ephesians prayer over yourself for wisdom and revelation regarding that event, change or blessing so God can show you how to embrace that blessing or change and pull it into your life.

If a person's face comes before you, you will pray the Ephesians prayer for him or her and see what comes to your heart. Pray blessings over that person and perhaps you will see yourself calling that person to encourage and bless him or her. Maybe you will see yourself baby-sitting a couple's children to give them a night off or giving someone in need money or just being a friend to someone.

Perhaps when specifically praying for another person, you will "sense" a shortcoming or weakness about that person—even a fault or a "flat out" sin. Perhaps it is something that person struggles with and is validly working to overcome. These tendencies or weaknesses may, in fact, be a "truth" about that person. However, if the Spirit of Truth is helping you, He will also remind you of Philippians 4:8. This scripture encourages New Testament saints not only to dwell on things that are *true*, but also to dwell on things that are of a *good report*, things that are *lovely, noble and praiseworthy*.

You see, if the Holy Spirit moves through you to help another dear saint, it will never be so you can gather with other saints to discuss a person's faults. The Holy Spirit will always lead you in prayer for others through the *law of love*. He will **never** pray apart from 1 Corinthians 13 because love never fails.

Truth be told, if we are following the Spirit of the Truth—even if we sense a weakness or sinful tendency in a person we pray about—we should *never* gossip about it or *wrap our own opinions around it.* The Spirit of the Truth, the Helper, will always inspire us with a scripture we can pray for that person. The Holy Spirit will lead us to wrap our faith and love around him or her. In fact, we should thank the Lord that the person stands fast in Him. After all, we should never judge another man's servant (our brothers and sisters are servants of the Lord). Those servants—whether they stand or fall—they stand or fall to the Lord. And the Lord is well able to make them stand (Romans 14:4).

Second Corinthians 3:6 says that the "letter" of the Bible without the Spirit kills. But, hallelujah, the Word and the Spirit and/or the Spirit of the Word makes alive evermore!

In this way, following the Spirit through the Word of God keeps us safe and effectual; following the Holy Spirit keeps us within the guardrails of love. That's monumentally important considering God *is* love (1 John 4:16).

Another important facet of Spirit-led prayer is to pray "clean." *What does that mean?* Let me explain. James 3 speaks of two kinds of wisdom. Verses 15 and 16 speak of a "wisdom that does not descend from above, but is earthly, sensual, and demonic. For where envy and self seeking exist, confusion and every evil thing will be there." Yet, when the Bible speaks of a wisdom that's "sensual," it's not speaking about a belly dancer or something erotic in nature. It's speaking about discerning things according to the five senses. It refers to discerning things according to our senses in the natural or the way things look— maybe even according to what *we want* to see happen. Nevertheless, we cannot pray that way for someone else's life. It's important to pray the "will of God" for people and situations—not our will.

Our natural emotions and mental understandings do not necessarily produce what God wants—so we must always stay in line with the Word of God with its "view" of things. God will always lead us in *triumph* with regard to ourselves and other peoples. His paths are always paths of peace and joy, and He makes a way where it looks like there is no way for people. He is ever ready to believe the best about anyone and everything. This is the mind of Christ.

Verse 17 of this same chapter in James goes on to describe the "attitude," and thus, the "spirit" that the Word of God will always produce in the work of prayer. Verse 17 says, "But the wisdom that is from *above* is first pure, then peaceable, gentle, willing to yield, full of mercy and good fruits, without partiality, and without hypocrisy."

Verse 18 so eloquently finishes up by saying, "Now the fruit of righteousness is sown in peace by those who make peace." The Spirit of the Word will never lead us outside the pathway of love. The blessed Trinity will always keep us on the blessed highway, the most excellent way of faith and love. Hallelujah!

Remember: Pray the Ephesians prayer, Ephesians 1:17-23, over yourself at the beginning of your prayer time. Then step out and pray in your understanding as subtle promptings, divine thoughts and leadings arise in your heart. Don't forget this simple format. I'm still a doer of this format to this very day. Prayer stays hot, vital, fun and **easy** for me and others who practice this way to pray. You will also **enjoy** your prayer time. You will leave prayer encouraged, invigorated and wanting more.

WORKING SIDE BY SIDE WITH THE HOLY GHOST

It is the joy of our lives to come to know the Spirit of God. It is an intimate place—a mature love—to let Him speak to us, correct us, mold us and shape us through His words. It is then another step altogether to follow Him into the place of prayer. It's in a place of prayer that we actually begin to do His words. We take the building blocks of His Word into prayer, and there we begin to build the kingdom of the Lord.

We learn so much about people when we live with them, and we also learn so much about people when we roll up our sleeves and actually work with them on a daily basis. We can all think of jobs where we've shared with co-workers the heat of the workday or times of urgency to get a job done quickly. We can all probably recall sharing the joys of a job well done or lunch breaks when thoughts, desires, concerns and joys were shared. We've even learned a lot after work hours just enjoying the company of co-workers and having fun.

Let me encourage you to continue on to know the Lord in this way. Pray the Ephesians prayer, and let the scriptures speak to you regarding your personal needs, your call and your purpose in life. But don't stop there! Take that training and preparation in His Word into the area of prayer and become a laborer together with Him. Take His yoke upon you for the work and blessing of prayer. Take on the work of building the kingdom with Him—side by side. Learn of His ways, His bidding,

His doings—learn of Him. In so knowing Him this way, you shall find a rest for your soul; as you learn of Him, you will trust Him more.

This is the relationship the mature Church will know. After all, saints, Jesus is coming back for a bride who is a **helpmeet**. Jesus is not coming back for a Church that is a newborn baby. Jesus is returning for a helper—*for a Church whose not only met Him, but has also taken the responsibility of working alongside Him.* This is the mature love and willful response He seeks. *Jesus is coming back for a kingdom-building partner, a companion, a co-laborer. He is coming for those who have yielded to, followed and learned the ways of the Helper.*

Hosea 6:3

"Let us know, Let us pursue the knowledge of the Lord. His going forth is established as the morning; He will come to us like the rain, Like the latter and former rain to the earth."

CHAPTER **12**

NOW **IT'S TIME** TO PRAY!

Ok, this is it! Get your Bible. Get a notebook. Get a pen because Psalm 45:1 says, "He, the Lord, hath made your tongue as the pen of a *ready* writer." Flip open your notebook and date a page. Maybe you should even get a recorder because things might get wild and really take off with you. Here goes.

It's time to pray!

Maybe you'll jot down notes while you're praying or after you've finished praying. But whether you are a "while-you-pray-kind" or "after-you-pray-kind" of person, be sure to write down what you feel the Lord directed you to pray about that day. As you "esteem" those subtle leadings the Lord may have given you, He will confirm, teach, illustrate, prompt and even quicken His leadings to you. Consequently, His leadings will become stronger as confirmations embolden and buoy your faith. You will begin to learn by faith how the Spirit of God speaks to *you!*

EXAMPLES OF HOW THE LORD SPEAKS

I want to share a few examples of how the Lord speaks to people, but keep in mind that these are only a few examples at best. After all, some people get words of knowledge (1 Corinthians 13), some people see pictures, some people just become conscious of individuals, situations, events, subjects, scriptures, nations, etc. I am honestly still learning what the gamut of unction truly includes.

Holy Ghost unction is as varied as the very definition of the word *leading*, and as broad as the truth of the *inward witness*. It's a quickening, an enduement, a download, a clarity, a compassion, a boldness, a joy, a dedication, a resolution, a consciousness, a peace and a knowing. Actually, I'm still working on my list as I continually discover new ways that He leads. Bottom line, however a Holy Ghost leading manifests to you on a given day, *write it down!*

Now for your Bible, open it to Ephesians 1:17-23.

You're ready! This is it.

First, pray the Ephesians prayer out loud. Mean it. Tell God you are expecting the spirit of wisdom and revelation in the knowledge of Him **to manifest as you pray**. Thank Him that your heart is being enlightened and you know the hope of His calling. Ask Him to reveal to you the glorious inheritance He has in the saints. Ask Him to let you know the exceeding greatness of His power and pray all the way to verse 23. Then, thank Him, thank Him, thank Him for speaking to you. I recommend you pray this prayer the very same way you prayed it before reading your Bible.

Then I would pray the following in some semblance of order every day: "Father God, I'm getting ready to pray so I come to You on the basis of Your Word. Jesus is the Word, and You have exalted His name above every name. You've said of Yourself that You have exalted Your Word above even Your own name. Therefore, if the Word of God is above Your own name, then for sure the Word of God is above my name. So I thank You that I am not praying in my name or by my ability. I am praying by Your ability, by your Spirit and by Your leadings within me.

"I am praying by faith in Your Word, therefore, I am following You. I do hear Your voice, and I am an effectual pray-er. I'm not just putting in time to pray to impress You or me. I thank You that because I am praying first Your Word—the Ephesians prayer—that I can and will have wisdom, revelation and knowledge of You today—right now as I pray.

"I will not just bumble around nebulously, confused, bored, burdened and bummed out! I receive wisdom and revelation and knowledge of You. My eyes **are enlightened, and I will know more of the hope of Your calling and of the very glorious inheritance on the inside of me."**

Dude: Here's the deal. You may just start shouting right in the middle of this prayer. I mean, sometimes I try with all my might just to finish the prayer. Even as I demonstrate this prayer to you, you can feel the Holy Ghost trying to rise up to pray—and quicken, make alive, make joyous and lead the way for you in prayer.

I continue on to the very end of the prayer, still baiting as it were and weighting my prayer with faith so the Holy Ghost may then *seize upon my lead* in my understanding. In other words because you did your part, the Holy Ghost is released to do His part. You stepped out in faith to pray in your understanding by strict submission to the scriptures and took the lead.

Now, the Holy Ghost can manifest His "helping!"

In response to your demonstrated faith, He will now begin to help you. He will take hold together with you because you're actually doing something by faith. In fact, He will do a whole lot more than take hold together with you in helping. Because you have done what is necessary to arouse, provoke and provide a sacrifice, He will now manifest and consume that sacrifice with His fiery leading. In divine sequence, you will be able to subtly shift your gears and follow His dynamic, unique, supernatural—if not almost spectacular—leading.

The effectual, fervent prayer of a righteous *man* makes *tremendous power arise and be made available.* The Holy Ghost has found someone humble enough to put the Word that He Himself wrote in the *first place.* So the great and mighty Spirit of God begins to brood and stir and swell and break into the very power and anointing that raised Jesus from the dead. Tremendous power and leading is building and being made available until suddenly clarity, unction and direction burst on the inside and break over your mind. It manifests itself in a dynamic—a leading, an unction, a knowing of which way to go, what to pray for and how to follow the great and mighty Spirit of Truth as worthily as we ought.

Continue praying the prayer in your understanding, if you can. You may sense the Holy Ghost rise up strong on the inside to ask for certain things, and you'll become very conscious of persons, situations, nations, etc. That's great! Still, just try to make it to the end of the prayer where the unction will be even stronger.

Ask boldly to experience and know the exceeding

greatness of His power, which He wrought in Christ when He raised Him from the dead. Ask to know more of it in your current prayer session. Ask now! Today is the day of salvation! Ask to know that power of the ages to come. **Ask to know more of Jesus who was given to be head of the Church.** And, of course, adamantly petition to know more of and how to flow better with His glorious and precious body, the very fullness of Him that shall fill all in (and through) all. (Side note: It wouldn't hurt if you shouted and rejoiced a little at this point like you really, might just, you know, believe it's actually happening at this very minute as you pray!)

Then dare to take off in your understanding!

Go ahead! Stretch out! Enjoy!

Take in the sights!

The very spirit of your mind has been washed with the Word. Your heart has been convinced and aligned with the power of the Word that is as sure as the very foundations of the world. You're safe! You're anchored! You're free and liberated to pray by faith!

So fly!

Pray in your understanding and see where you go!

Pray this prayer every day. As you do His leadings will teach you. Each day He will lead you a different way. It is the *diversity* of the Spirit. It is a *manifestation* of the Spirit to teach us all His plans and purposes. Actually, 1 Corinthians 12:6-7 and 11 encourages us in this spirit walk and says, "There are **diversities** of activities, but it is the **same God** who works **all in all**.

But the **manifestation** of the Spirit is given to **each one** for the profit of **all**. But one and the same Spirit works all these things, distributing to **each one individually** as **He wills**."

PRAYER ADVENTURES

Let's consider a few prayer adventures in order to demonstrate practical examples of how Spirit-led prayer might flow.

Let's say one day after praying the Ephesians prayer, you have a strong sense to pray for the president. Or maybe one day after praying the Ephesians prayer, you remember seeing a news report on a situation in Korea so you pray about that.

Then again, perhaps the next time you pray it's totally different. Let's say while standing in line at the grocery store you see an ad for impoverished children in the Appalachian Mountains. The ad strikes you so you buy the magazine. Then upon praying the Ephesians prayer again the next day, you're suddenly conscious of the Appalachian children. You pray for them again. You are amazed those children came right up on the inside of you. Your heart still captivated, maybe the next day you stop by a major bookstore to buy a book on the Appalachian Mountains because somehow they seem so intriguing to you. For some reason, you just want to read more about them.

Since prayer is full of adventure, you may not have two days alike. So maybe the next day after praying the Ephesians prayer, a neighbor's name comes up in your spirit and so does—oh, my goodness—a scripture or a part of one. You wonder, *Is this really, truly a scripture or have I seen that phrase in Reader's Digest or maybe on a Hallmark card?* If it's really a scripture, you wonder where in the Bible it's found, but still you immediately write down, " **...and God makes all things work together for the good....**" After prayer you dare to look it up in a concordance.

Just in case you're wondering, *What is this thing called a concordance?* Here's the scoop. A concordance is a big fat book you can buy in a Bible bookstore, which includes all the words included in every scripture of the Bible. Say, for example, that you wanted to study about *healing.* Well, you would open your concordance and look up any words you could think of that have to do with healing, and it will show you scriptures that contain that word or subject. For example, you would look up *heal, healed, healing, health, healeth,* etc.

(FYI, I would get an "exhaustive" concordance, which means it contains all the words you'll ever need. Actually, it's exhausting not only in the number of words in the book, but also just to carry the thing from one room to another. Let's just say an exhaustive concordance is gi-normous. In fact, I was on a mission trip to Africa, and a roach the size of an RV crawled across my floor. In my haste I dropped my Strong's Concordance on it, and the concordance smashed him thoroughly. Thus, you get the size of my concordance.)

Back to our prayer example, did you find that "piece" of scripture you got in prayer? Well, what do you know—it's actually in the Bible. You're becoming quite the whiz or scholar. You're also beginning to see how the One who wrote the Bible and lives on the inside of you will teach, lead and show you what that baby called the Bible is built to do. I bet you'll find your piece of scripture is a part of a verse in Romans 8. WOW!

So you go to your Bible and read the portion of scripture in context. That is, you read the previous chapter and the chapter following the verse. Your verse is found in Romans 8:28, "And we know that all things work together for good to those who love God, to those who are called according to His purpose." WOW again! What a blessing that scripture is, and the Holy Ghost gave it to you. You discover the whole chapter is even in context talking about the blessings of praying in line with the will of God. **Severe coolness!** You just prayed out a blessing for you. And whoa—already you got blessed.

You begin to recognize that as you are praying by the help of the Holy Ghost, God causes all things—even things that are bad—to work out for your good. Wow—you've never seen that scripture like that before! Actually, maybe before this day you had never even seen that scripture at all. You're so impressed with the Holy Ghost! In fact, it's as though Someone—who knew scriptures really well—perhaps even Someone who wrote the scriptures is on the inside of you leading and guiding you through the writings of the Bible. The Holy Spirit wrote the scriptures, and He knows what you need.

Well Someone "greater" in knowledge of the Word than you *is* living on the inside of *you*—teaching and instructing you regarding this historical library of old. It's as though that scripture just leaped out of the page at you and spoke to you. That scripture had an authority and even a volume that impacted you. You feel invigorated, strengthened and really encouraged.

Awesome! Wow! You leave the place of prayer elated.

You're amazed that you have not been watching the clock—you have been "watching and praying"—watching, that is, for a leading, a blessing, a revelation. You are rejuvenated. Your prayer time has not been a time of worry, struggle or work. It has been a blessed time of following the witness of the Holy Ghost to nations, people, events and it spills over into a big splash of encouragement for your own life. You're so encouraged you're now saying, "Dude, surf's up in my life. I'm catching waves, dude. It's awesome. I think I will go buy some spray-on tanning solution and highlight my hair, dude. It's that awesome!"

So, the next day you pray the Ephesians prayer once again. You know it by heart now even though certain parts of the prayer itself seem to jump out at you. You camp on certain words that just seem to bless you. Perhaps the phrase, *"His glorious inheritance in the saints"* strikes you. So you camp there. You begin to revel in the fact that He has placed an inheritance of the very glory of God within you. As you speak this out, you can sense a quickening in your very physical body as you release and or acknowledge this good thing within you. The peace of God manifests. That headache leaves, pain leaves, worry and care leave.

Perhaps the Holy Spirit brings to your remembrance Colossians 1:27, which says, " ... Christ in *you*, the hope of glory!" You realize that Jesus, the Christ, the Son of God who went about doing good and healing all who were oppressed by the devil abides on the inside of you in His very glory. You're simply an earthen vessel, but Glory has made His home in you. Woo hoo! You're so healed and strengthened you almost can't stand it.

On this healing wave come even more scriptures. You read, "God is the strength of my heart... " (Psalm 73:26). "Be strong in the Lord and in the power of His might... " (Ephesians 6:10). "...The joy of the Lord is my strength" (Nehemiah 8:10). My, my, my, the avenues of revelation and blessing are truly endless, even eternal. Your prayer time with Him becomes a veritable "gold mine" of blessing in every tangent and at every turn.

As you continue to pray, perhaps you become conscious of your pastor so you pray the Ephesians prayer for him or her. Just as the woman with the oil anointed Jesus' head, just as the woman with the perfume washed Jesus' feet, you begin to anoint your pastor and wash his "feet" in prayer with the water of the Word. You take the Ephesians prayer and begin to call out and thank the Lord that your pastor has the spirit of wisdom and revelation in the knowledge of Him. You pray that your dear pastor's eyes are enlightened and that he or she knows the hope of Jesus calling.

You take a tangent by the Holy Ghost and begin to add another prayer. You add Ephesians 3, praying your pastor be strengthened with might in the inner man to grasp and apprehend that which God has called him or her to. You begin to thank God for your pastor in accordance with 1 Timothy 2:11-2, which tells us to pray for leaders with prayers and thanksgivings.

As you're praying you recall Ephesians 6:18-19 and you request with thanksgiving that your pastor has supernatural utterance and boldness to make known the mystery of the plan of God for your church. Ooops! Wait! The Holy Spirit nudges you so you look at the clock only to realize you've got to hurry to get to work or you'll be late. You leave for work edified and destined to reap blessing as you have just been a sower of blessings.

Hmmm—you make a mental note to self. After praying for your pastor that way, you suddenly have a desire to get more involved in serving at the church or to give your pastor and spouse a gift card to a really nice restaurant. Bottom line: You start walking in a pathway of sowing and blessing that will set you on a pathway of reaping the blessings of God as never before.

The next day you start again with your old friend the Ephesians prayer. You are bathing in the very blessing it is to pray this mighty prayer. You follow that stream for a while, and then, oh my goodness, suddenly the children of Appalachia are once again before your eyes. The image of them comes so strong this time. You think, *Well, I guess I will lift up those children in Appalachia once again.* Compassion rises up in you. This is not like you; you're not even a crier. Yet, the mercies of God well up and roll down your cheeks. You cry out for those kids. The spirit of wisdom and revelation in the knowledge of Jesus rises up and the knowledge and wisdom of what Jesus wants done to help them. In your heart you envision God wanting to raise up churches in the area to reach out to them. You envision orphanages, and you envision the gospel and finances reaching out to that area. Such vision! Such possibility!

Tomorrow comes and prayer begins again anew. Daily you continue to pray the Ephesians prayer and follow whatever leading He gives you. But something just keeps rising up about those kids. It's getting so strong you can barely stand it. You begin to seek out organizations that supply aid to the children in that area and organizations you can support. You write checks and send them, which "relieves" the passion in your heart somewhat. But rats—it keeps getting stronger and stronger!

When other people talk about outreaches, you pipe up and suggest outreaches to the Appalachian Mountain children. Some think it's a good idea; others are not so hot about it. You find yourself starting to get a little defensive—even protective or a little mad—because everyone doesn't see this revelation and purpose the way you do. Yet because you know that scriptures say "love does not take offense" in 1 Corinthians 13, you become quiet and ponder these things.

Actually you begin to wonder, *What's the deal with me and these children I cannot shake?* The deal is that you are caring about that group of people or that subject like healing or prosperity. Like a child who has been born through you, you are "carrying" those people or that subject. It becomes your baby, so to speak, and you carry it, nurture it and are continually conscious of it. The reality is that you have seen how God views this given topic, and you are carrying His heart about it. It is not for another; it is a piece of the call of God for *you!*

Well, you wonder, *Maybe I should go on a trip to help those mountain children in some way?* Perhaps you will. But at this juncture just keep praying the Ephesians prayer around it, and you'll know the next step. Keep thanking God for the next step all the while realizing "the steps of a good man are ordered of the Lord" (Psalm 37:23). Ephesians 2:10 says, "There are works God ordained for us to walk in before the foundations of the earth—that we *should* walk in them." By faith, thank God that you *are* walking in the works He predestined for you.

Revelation will get stronger about whatever repeatedly comes up in your heart—those peoples, subjects, nations, businesses, careers, work or whatever. First revelation comes then the faith to do the work follows. And the more you pray, the stronger your love becomes until His love courses through you with regard to a given people, work or subject. Love will get so strong until you cannot stand it anymore—then, you arise, you go do, and you manifest the plan and purpose of God.

Love has caused your faith to rise up and work, and nothing is impossible to you now. You've come to see and recognize your inheritance in Christ—those peoples or that work—which were all the time inside you, but now are manifesting to the glory of God. Hallelujah!

There's the vision, my friend.

All the while your love *is* getting so strong. As you yield yourself to pray, this mighty prayer on the lips of the Holy Spirit sheds or pours out the love of Christ in your heart. You are becoming like our Lord. God has so much compassion that it says over and over again in the Gospels, Jesus was *moved* with compassion. Yet now, your vision born of faith and spawned by God's *wisdom* and *revelation* begins to *work by love.* Your love begins to abound and extend into a comprehensive wisdom and knowledge. You are starting to know where you can help and what He wants you to do.

It should come as no surprise that before long you plan a trip to Appalachia to see those children who captivated your heart. It's no surprise at all! God arranges divine connections so you "just happen" to meet a group of Christians planning to do the same thing. You were very aware that it did not seem like you would have the finances to go. Yet, you trusted the Lord who told you to go. All of the sudden, other people came up to you prompted by the Lord Himself and joyfully financed the entire trip and then some. Your financial provision came in. Even your family was affected toward God because of the mighty momentum of His presence in your life.

You are acting totally different. It is as though it is no longer you that liveth, but Christ Himself taking up residence and living His life and plans through you. You hear His voice. You ask Him to bring to pass these things you see in your heart. He answers you and brings them to pass. The works and projects do not fail—you do not fail—because love never fails.

Your works are not done in vain, but your works are a fruit of the Spirit because they were authored by revelation and wisdom. They were conceived and fueled by God's love in you. So follow your love; it's safe now to follow your passion. It is the blueprint of His plans for you.

You begin to realize that it's so easy to find God's plans, His purposes and His pursuits because they are on the inside of each one of us. Yes, He is on the inside of us. When we offer Him what He wants—the Word of God on our lips prayed to Him—the very power of the Word blended with the person of the

Holy Spirit reveals to us what is already present in our spirit man: *His plans and purposes for our lives.*

Perhaps He is calling you to a subject. For instance, some people are provoked by the Holy Spirit to investigate the subject of divine healing. Go ahead and attach the Ephesians prayer to this subject saying, "Father, I ask You for the spirit of wisdom and revelation in the knowledge of You regarding *healing*!" Then Let Him unfurl revelation of just what did happen at the Cross and the price that was paid for every sickness and disease to be swallowed up by life. From a cold to AIDS, it does not matter. The answer to healing is always *yes!* You pray the Ephesians prayer over yourself and then head toward the Gospels to watch Jesus heal people. Maybe you will even study healing from the Gospel of Luke—Luke was a physician after all.

Perhaps you made it to Luke 8:43 where the passage jumps out at you: " ...*a woman with an issue of blood 12 years....*" You read where the woman saw Jesus and said within herself, "If I but touch the hem of His garment, I will be made whole." You're captivated reading how she pressed through to touch His garment and virtue goes out of Jesus to heal her. You realize the woman touched the hem of His garment, and even before Jesus had died on the Cross and the power of the resurrection had been released, she was healed.

Revelation bursts on the inside of you! Suddenly on the inside you recognize "a knowing" in response to this scripture. You realize, "Hey, I am a Christian. I identify with Jesus *now after* He died on the Cross and the power of the resurrection is released. And now, I am *always* touching Him because He is always *in me.* Therefore, that virtue, that healing life of God, is constantly being emanated throughout my organs, my skin, my bones, my blood—all my flesh. The scriptures are showing me that I am healed. No matter what it looks like or feels like, the Word is showing me, teaching me, imparting to me vision and a revelation that I am healed." Then as you see it, your body is quickened!

But there's more! As healing is manifesting in your body, you're even more determined to keep praying this prayer and reading your Bible. Hmmm. You not only see yourself healed, but you also see yourself laying hands on the sick. You recall that scripture that says believers would lay hands on the sick (Mark 16:18). Are you amazed? Not only is the Word quickening your body, but now it's also writing down a job description of something you are called to do. Wow!

Consider another example of how prayer can flow. Perhaps when you pray you're drawn to the Bible subject of *prosperity.* Is it any wonder? After all, you are tired of poverty. The Bible agrees with you that poverty is a curse. In Luke 4:18-19 Jesus said His calling was to "preach good news to the poor." What is good news to the poor? The good news is that they "ain't gotta be po-no-mo!" That's what you call really good news! Perhaps you've never been poor, but have a desire to give amazing amounts of money into the work of the gospel. Well then, pray the Ephesians prayer regarding that as well. Pray like this: "Father, I ask for the spirit of wisdom and revelation in the knowledge of You regarding prosperity." Let Him show you realms of liberality that will amaze the world.

God the Father will let you fellowship with Him and partake of His miraculous giving nature. Want to really see a giver? You already have—God gave His only begotten Son for you. Fellowship and talk with Him, and He will show you how this was done. Learn the nature and power of such selfless love. Let Him form and fashion you into His very image, and we will see another on the earth just like Him. We'll see *you* giving in such a way that it's as a sign and wonder.

Like Him, like He gave His Son, we'll see you

Just like Him, such a giver, just like Him, you are

another one!

We'll see you giving so generously, so unselfishly, that it

is a sign and a wonder.

Yes—miraculous giving, supernatural generosity.

God the Father will put the very nature of His fatherhood in you, causing you to yearn to provide for others. That nature will cause you to yearn to fund, support, lavish and bless. Then as you catch the vision of the business He is inspiring, the very revelation itself will inspire divine connections. Favor will open doors for you; people will be drawn to help you.

As you study the Abrahamic blessing in Galatians 3:13, you'll be even more convinced that prosperity is most certainly the will of God. Heaven is not gold-plated; heaven is *made of gold—it is the* basic element and building block of eternity. Truth is, Jesus told Christians to *"go ye"!* But in today's world, to "go ye" costs bucks, baby. Airline tickets, buildings, licenses, chairs, outreach, they all cost bucks. Bucks are not evil; money is not evil. The Bible says it's the *love of money* that's the root of all evil.

So as you pray the Ephesians prayer and study the scriptures regarding prosperity, not only will you recognize that Jesus' blood paid for your prosperity, but divine ideas also will come to you suddenly. A business, a method, an invention or even a "way" of giving will come to you. As you pray the Ephesians prayer in the light of the written Word, you'll see as you've never seen before. You'll see the light of what you are called to do.

Second Corinthians 8:9 says, "That though He [Jesus] was rich, yet for our sakes, He was made poor, that we through His poverty, would be made rich." You are reminded that in 2 Corinthians 9:8 it says, "My God is able to make all grace (every favor and earthly blessing come to you in abundance...)" (AMP). So you head off to your job, not trying to beat out the other guy because you have favor.

Your God is supplying all your needs, opening doors for you that no man can close. You are laboring in faith, and in return, God is giving you grace, great favor and earthly blessings such as salary increases, investment tips and even bonuses. Grace and favor cover you, the blessing of Abraham sits on you, and everywhere you go you are a portrait of blessing. Your profiting is evident to all!

As we pray the Ephesians prayer we line up in faith to hear from God, and as we dare to pray what we believe God is saying to us we launch out in faith. Woo hoo! When faith comes on the scene, we are no longer limited by the mental realm. We are moving and movable. We let the Lord move us to pray for this and that, and then suddenly we find ourselves drawn, led toward and yielding to what God has actually destined us to do.

CHAPTER **13**

THE **INDISPENSABLE** INWARD WITNESS

Some people depend on scholarly philosophies to guide them through life. Some people depend on detailed maps. Others look to wisdom handed down from generation to generation. But you—if you're a born-again, Spirit-filled Christian—have help way beyond earthly platitudes. You have the Creator of the universe—the author of the Bible, the very power of God—living in you and guiding you through life. You have the Holy Spirit—the indispensable inward witness—inside you.

As you've been faithful to pray the Ephesians prayer before your times of Bible study and prayer and write down scriptures and promptings of the Lord, you've found the *inward witness* of the Lord becoming stronger and stronger in you. It's as though Someone totally turned up the volume button in your heart. After all, His Words have broken open on the inside of you and now they literally abide in you. You've followed the Holy Spirit through God's Word and through prayer, and you've become more and more acquainted with the voice of God, the leadings of God and the very attitude and personality of God. You've come to personally and intimately know the witness of His Spirit.

1 John 5:6 says, "It is the Spirit Who *bears witness* because the Spirit is truth." As a result, this witness in our hearts will:

Make us a witness to others

and

lead and guide us in the daily affairs, major decisions,

and plans and purposes of God for our lives.

John 15:26 says, "But when the Comforter is come, whom I will send unto you from the Father, even the Spirit of truth, which proceedeth from the Father, He shall testify of Me. And ye also, *shall bear witness*...." The *same Spirit* who leads us through the Word and prayer via the Ephesians prayer is the *same Spirit* who leads us through our daily lives. He comforts us *through the inward witness; He leads us by the inward witness.*

After the resurrection and just prior to His ascension, the Lord Jesus told us more about how the great and mighty Holy Spirit would help us. Acts 1:8 says, "But you shall *receive power* when the Holy Spirit has come upon you, and you shall be *witnesses* to Me in Jerusalem, and in all Judea and Samaria, and to the end of the Earth."

As we follow the Holy Spirit, He will bear witness showing us how we are to witness and to whom we should witness. The Holy Spirit will bear witness regarding which way to go when we make decisions. In fact, He's very practical. He will bear witness as to what cars we should buy or where to apply for a job, what business to start or investment to undertake. He'll even bear witness as to where our car keys are as we scurry around hunting for them.

Our Helper is absolutely amazing. He will bear witness showing parents how to discipline one child as opposed to another. He will bear witness regarding what to say and what not to say. How valuable is that? He will bear witness concerning how to have favor with others regarding the plans and purposes of God. Oh yeah. And He will bear witness about what you are called to do in life, where you are to live and how you are to walk in all the blessings of God.

Jesus did not say, "Listen here, you had better hit the streets and win one person a day to Me, or I'll hit you with a lightning bolt or run over you with a Hummer." No! Jesus in His great mercy does not threaten you to witness to others. He simply says that if you follow Him you will do a lot more than witness—*you'll become a witness*. You will be a beacon, a living epistle known and read of all men.

Actually, Jesus wants you to become a testimony in your daily walk. Following the Holy Spirit on a day-to-day basis will draw all men to you and ultimately to Him, the Lord Jesus Christ. In Matthew 4:19 Jesus told us simply, "**Follow me**, and I will **make** you fishers of men." Quit trying to be a Christian and quit trying to be the chief witnesser. Just follow that inward witness, and Jesus will make you into a first-class witness. You'll come to know joy unspeakable as you follow His Spirit. He will lead you to intersect the lives of the downtrodden with His reality and power.

AN 'AMAZING' DRUNK AND HIGH GIRL

One night a while back when I lived in an apartment, I was very late getting home from a meeting. That wasn't exactly a plus because parking was limited. Unfortunately, that night the parking lot was completely full, which meant I had to parallel park on the street. Yuck!

I prayed, fasted, quoted the Word and bound devils in my attempt to get close to the curb and fit into a really tight space. As soon as I was finished, here came another car pulling up near a supposed space. It was such a tiny spot and I thought, *There's no way that car will fit in there!* Wrong. The driver began parking with the accuracy of a surgeon and the speed and boldness of a stunt car driver. Quickly the car launched forward, then abruptly stopped. Backed in. Wheels turned a little forward—*then bam.* Done! Like putting a ship into a bottle or a whale into a banana skin, that car was in that spot. My eyes were riveted.

It was late at night, and I was tired. I had ministered and prayed for many people during that night's service, and I just wanted to get into my apartment to pray, sleep and replenish. But for some reason this parking demonstration was so amazing to me—so fascinating, so interesting. For some reason, I had to see what the driver looked like. *He must be a professional driver or a race car person, maybe a mechanic,* I thought.

Guess what? The car door opened and out *stumbled* a girl. She was scantily clad and obviously drunk—high even—and could barely walk. This girl got out of the car and staggered up to her apartment. *I was amazed!* Here was a girl clearly under the influence who'd been able to park like that.

She should never have been behind the wheel, of course. But my job was not to go rebuke her—after all, the gospel is good news. Jesus did not come to the earth to condemn the earth or point out to sinners when they were sinning. No, Jesus came to seek, save and tell the lost that they don't have to stop sinning; they simply have to give their lives to Him. Sin won't be a problem when Jesus is in a person's life.

Still, I was amazed. Here I had almost called a prayer chain to get help to park my vehicle. I was stone cold sober, and still, it was difficult for me to park. Yet, again, for some reason, I was absolutely, totally amazed.

A few days later I was running out of my apartment busy with the "work of the Lord," so to speak. I had a whole list of church stuff to do—meetings and more meetings and dinners and fellowships to attend. Busy, busy, busy I was. In the midst of rushing to my car, I glanced over and saw a girl sitting on the front stoop of the apartment complex. She was wearing a top that didn't cover much, sporting several tattoos and smoking a cigarette.

Even in my rush, I suddenly seemed to have a revelation or a consciousness that this girl was the "amazing driver girl"—the amazing drunk and high girl—who had parked with such skill. I was busy. I was not thinking about sharing my faith; I was not pondering who that girl was who had parked like that a few days before. Yet, I found myself wondering, " *Hmmm, is that the girl who parked so well a few days ago? Maybe I should go talk to her about the Lord? Nah, I am busy. I've got kingdom business to do. Nah.*

Still, why was I noticing her so much? Why was I wondering if she was the "parking girl"? Why had the parking experience been so highlighted or interesting to me? Why was I even having an inward dialogue about this girl whom I did not know and really didn't necessarily want to know? I mean, I'm busy. Plus, she looked pretty rough. What if she stabbed me? No, she was more likely to think I'm crazy, I concluded. Honestly, it would be awkward just to walk up to her, I reasoned.

With all these thoughts swirling around in my mind, I notice that my footsteps slowed. I hesitated getting into my car. Yup,you guessed it. The Ephesians prayer was holding me up. Oh yeah.

I had committed to a lifestyle of prayer and had been faithfully praying the Ephesians prayers before I studied my Bible. I was well exercised at letting scriptures be highlighted to me and letting the Holy Spirit teach me about the scriptures. I had prayed the Ephesians prayers at the beginning of my prayer time and then prayed in my understanding. I had let the Holy Spirit draw me and prompt me. And as a result— right here and right now—the Holy Spirit was leading me in life. The rubber had met the road, so to speak.

At that moment in my daily walk, my heart was trained to respond to the leading and guidance of the Holy Spirit. Suddenly He was prompting and drawing me to this girl. She had become *highlighted* to me. The Holy Ghost was bearing witness on the inside of me as I looked at her and thought about her. I knew if I would respond to His prompting by simply going over to talk to her, the voice of the Lord and His promptings would get stronger in every area of my life.

Incoming bulletin of a supernatural sort! Major point here: *The same Holy Spirit that leads and guides you through the Word of God and through prayer is the same Spirit who empowers you to minister to others. Follow Jesus as He bears witness through His Spirit, and He will* **make you a witness.**

So sensing that the Holy Spirit was drawing me to "amazing driver girl," I *decided to act* on the *prompting*. It was the same act of faith I exercised when I *decided to let* the Holy Ghost highlight scriptures to me. It was the same bold-yet-daring-woo-hoo-shaking-kind-of-nervous-hope-this-is-right-it-seems-like-it-might-be-right-even-though-I-don't-know-for-sure-in-my-head sort of feeling. Thoughts clanged around in my head: *My heart seems to like it, but my flesh doesn't want to be embarrassed. I'm taking a risk, but maybe I'll just step out in faith getting over the "I don't knows" and trusting God that I do hear His voice and that I am following and obeying Him.*

Despite the devil shouting, "Are you crazy?" in one ear, and despite my own lazy apathy in the other ear suggesting, "Go eat some Haagen Daz ice cream and watch a movie," I decided to obey my heart. Woo hoo for those who obey their hearts! Woo hoo! Because that's where the exploits are. That's where the blessings are, and that's where the intimacy of knowing the Lord is the strongest. When you obey Him, you can sense His pleasure, His power, His love and His joy.

So I walked up to "amazing driver girl," and of

course, she looked at me like I was insane. Be assured of this one thing. No matter how people look at you if the Holy Ghost is leading you to talk to someone, He knows what to say. He will lead you, and you will be effective even if they threaten to kill you. Do not regard their faces. Don't you know that people under conviction are sometimes the meanest people you'll ever meet?

In myself I did not know what to say, but I was not trusting in myself. I was trusting if I opened my mouth, the Bear Witness-er would fill it. I was trusting in the *Bear Witness-er* to help me *witness*. He got me into this, and He would get me through it.

I didn't try to say anything fancy to the girl. I just walked up and said, "Are you the girl who came in late a while back and despite being very wasted still parked your car with the skill of a surgeon?"

She seemed to like that and said, "Yes!"

"Well," I continued, "I am a Christian, and as I was walking to my car I felt prompted by the Lord to come talk to you."

Boy, I had her attention for sure, and it was sort of odd too. Instead of looking shocked or mad, she looked like I was speaking in such a way that was not foreign to her. I suddenly found myself thinking that maybe she had known the Lord before or perhaps she had family members who were Christians. When I acted on that "knowing," she let me know that she indeed had fallen away from the Lord a while back.

It was nothing spectacular; I just happened to

note her reaction. But, in fact, that is how the Holy Spirit shows us things and informs us. It is revelation, and it's so *supernatural* that you might just think it's you. Yet, the real point is that you have grown so in tune with the Holy Spirit that you can hardly tell the difference between Him and you. His Word is so abiding in you that your desires and thoughts are synonymous with His.

Just like in John 15:7, His words are abiding so much in you that His desires have become your desires. And, therefore, whatever you ask or say or do, it shall be accompanied and confirmed by His presence for it's His presence that initiated it in the first place. The last part of the verse also comes into play. John 15:8 goes on to promise us, "...so shall you bear fruit, [The fruit of the earth is the harvest of souls in the earth. Fruit is for someone else to eat and get blessed.] so shall the Lord be glorified, so shall you really become a *disciple*."

A disciple is someone who has been "disciplined," exercised and trained in the ways of righteousness. That's us! As we train our hearts to follow the Holy Spirit through the Word and prayer, we've disciplined our heart in the ways of God. We've allowed ourselves to be disciplined and **discipled** by the Spirit of God. Therefore, we qualify to "go and make disciples of all nations." Not only do we qualify, but also our hearts are so like that of the Lord that we are not satisfied doing anything else. Hallelujah, bless the name of the Lord.

So as I noted the reaction of "amazing driver girl," I continued to talk with her. I followed on to ask her of her background. "What's your deal? Are you a Christian? Have you ever known Jesus?" I asked.

Amidst her puffs of cigarette and from behind her multitudes of tattoos, she began to describe how she was a Christian and used to be on fire for God. She said that she and her mother were so in love with the Lord and were serving Him fervently, but then her mother had gotten sick—really sick....

From there I knew on the inside what had happened. Actually, you do too. Just as you are reading this, your spirit tells you what happened. She and her mother were so close, but her mother had gotten sick. This girl stood by her mother's side and continued to pray for her mother's healing, yet her mother died. In the midst of her hurt, she had become disillusioned and eventually went back into the world and its ways. The cigarettes and the drunkenness were not the core of the problem. It never is. They're just symptoms.

So many preachers just go after the symptoms and never after what makes God's children do those things. The reality is that cigarettes and drunkenness won't harm a person nearly as much as a broken heart and disillusionment will. The latter two are the deadly ones.

What about her mother, you ask? Well, physical healing is in the atonement. Jesus bore our sickness and carried our pains. Acts 10:38 says that Jesus went about *doing good* and healing. Healing is good; Jesus did and is doing a whole lot of it.

In Luke 13, Jesus described a woman bowed over in pain, saying, "Satan hath bound her...." Is there sickness in heaven? No. Jesus prayed, "Thy will be done on earth as it is in heaven" (Matthew 6:10). Healing is for today, friend.

Then how come all are not healed? you wonder.

How come all are not saved? I answer.

Jesus paid the price for our salvation, yet is everyone saved? Does everyone accept His free gift? No. Still, the gift of salvation is available whether it's accepted or not. We cannot base the blessing of salvation on whether or not other people get saved; we base salvation on what the Word of God says. And so it is with healing. We must continue to believe and stand for healing even if some do not get healed.

In reality, I did not know fully what was going on in the situation with "amazing driver girl's" dear mother. Perhaps she had gotten hold of erroneous doctrine, which disabled her from believing fully for her healing. Perhaps she had grown weary of the fight of faith. Perhaps she had just wanted to be with her Savior for the fight was too much for her. We should never judge people—pain is a terrible thing, and we have not walked in the shoes of another. No matter what the heart scenario, the woman was a Christian and so at worst she was walking the streets of glory even as we spoke.

The point is, we cannot know what is in another's heart. In this situation and in most situations, God will not reveal the inside story or inner workings of what happened. We don't need to know—it's between God and the individual.

Even in this situation, God did not speak to me about the mother's condition; the Lord was only prompting me about this young girl. It was not my job to root around and find out the details of the whole story. It was simply my job to deliver the message, and the Holy Spirit would take it from there.

It's not even that girl's job to figure it all out. So many people say, "I cannot go on with the Lord until I get this or that question answered. I will go no further until this or that is resolved." But that's not your job! Just purpose to follow the Lord day by day, and put your questions in a "faith drawer" or on a "faith shelf." Keep your faith pinned to your questions—trusting God to eventually reveal more light on the subject. But don't stop following on in the Lord. That is not faith, and you will never know what you want to know if you don't follow on. Hosea 6:3 says, " ... then shall we know, if we follow on to know the Lord...."

I told "amazing driver girl" that I was so sorry about her mother, and I also told her that the Lord had sent me to talk to her because He loved her and had a plan for her. I told her that He had been yearning for her and following her all these days.

"Can I just pray for you?" I asked.

You see, if you'll just lay your hand on a person and begin to pray in faith for him or her even if you have no idea what to say, you'll be amazed at what comes out. That is faith.

Man, I remember this story like it happened yesterday. I put my hand on her shoulder, and all of a sudden, compassion rolled up out of my heart. It was not just sad feelings like at a movie or when a person gets hurt; this was compassion of overwhelming love. More than sympathy, it was a divine empathy of identifying with her hurt, bitterness, loss and hopelessness. I felt the love of God so great for her that it shook my voice, welled up through my eyes and down my cheeks. That compassion went on to proclaim God's love and His plan and purpose for her.

As I finished praying and took my hand from her, I could see a "tangible peace" upon her. This peace was like a force around and upon her; her very face seemed to change. It was a peace not as the world gives, but the peace Jesus touted that only He could give. It was a peace that passes up the understanding and mounts a garrison like an impenetrable fortress over her mind and heart. It would keep her; it would guide her.

She was forever changed, and so was I. Once again the pipe or hose that carries the water to refresh someone else gets wet and gets a dose too! Before I left I got her phone number and talked to her about moving out to California where a church was beginning that I would attend. She said she would check it out.

As I headed back to my car the Holy Ghost did one more thing. He witnessed to my heart, "Go back and give her $20."

"No, no, no way!" she said when I walked toward her with the money.

"Oh yes, yes, yes way!" I said. "The same prompting that brought me over here to say also wants me to help *pay.*" I left her staunchly affected by the Lord Jesus Christ. Hallelujah!

Then, I went back to "church business." Ha, ha. When you think about it, what business could have been more important? Winning the lost is the true business of the Church, and you and I must be about our Father's business!

A BIKER WITH DRIER SHEETS

Have you ever used a Laundromat and tried to keep your undergarments under wraps in the process? (OK, you're probably wondering what this has to do with prayer, but bear with me.) You see, during my years at Bible school, I learned some valuable lessons at the Laundromat. And I'm about to share one of them with you.

One day at the Laundromat, I was doing my best to hide my underpants as I transferred them from washing machine to drier. When folding time came my diversion was to yell out: "Look, can you see? It's a three-toed sloth loading a Victorian catapult!" Or, "Hey isn't that the ShamWow guy? Look he's using paper towels. What's up with that? Are you following me camera guy?" Or, "Wow, can you see that? It's a dog that plays poker. He ain't no good, though—every time he's got a good hand, he wags his tail." Needless to say, these diversions are listed in the dictionary as definitions for the word *lame*. They did not work, and unfortunately many people viewed my undergarments. I hope there are no pictures on the Internet.

Anyway, so there I was at the Laundromat. I saw this guy doing his laundry who was not what you call a regular Laundromat person. He was decked out in motorcycle gear, leather head to foot. Just for the record, he also seemed to have a lot of body hair. Just saying. I might also add that he had one of those chains attached to his wallet, which in light of a very determined criminal would in effect only leave a guy "pantsless" and still minus his wallet. He may even have had a tattoo there somewhere. Have I made the point yet that normally this was not a person I would strike up a conversation with since he intimidated me a bit?

Hang on; there's more. Suddenly, I just happened to look down at the guy's laundry basket only to see that he had brought detergent (like really good, expensive detergent), *fabric softener and drier sheets.* Did you get that? Fabric softener and drier sheets! I don't know why, but this struck me as very ironic and comical. In my wonderment and amazement, all intimidation left me.

As though beside myself, I walked boldly up to him and asked, "Why do you have fabric softener and drier sheets, if you are a big tough biker?"

I honestly don't remember his answer. But as he began to speak, I could see that he was a really nice guy who simply liked to ride bikes and wear leather. Something else happened to me as he began to speak; I began to "come to my senses." Why had I suddenly crossed the room to speak to this individual? What was the purpose of this sudden interruption in my laundry process?

The guy sort of laughed at my question as he spoke, and all of the sudden on the inside of me *I just knew something.* I don't know how I knew, but I suddenly became *aware of something* or *conscious of something.* Or, really I just started wondering something and so I asked him, "Is anyone in your family a Christian?"

Boy oh boy, his whole countenance changed. He kind of hemmed and hawed around, became sheepish and embarrassed, then just "fessed up." "Why yes," he said, "my parents are preachers."

Ooohhhh, I got what was going on!

The great and mighty Holy Spirit—the third person of the Trinity and member of the Godhead who raised Jesus from the dead, the arm of God who created the universe, the Paraclete, the Holy Ghost—caused me to find this guy's laundry detergent regime interesting so that I'd go over and talk to him. This amazing **unconscious** leading of simply finding his use of fabric softener interesting—even amusing—turned into a powerful doorway of utterance and revelation whereby prayers of his family were answered as I reminded him that Jesus loves him and had a powerful ministry and plan for his life.

Something so close, seemingly natural and mundane as me finding his use of fabric softener funny was, in fact, the prompting of the Savior of the universe to bring home, call back and send this biker a message: "Come home to Father's house!" It was probably the faithfulness of the Lord as his parents had been calling out for their son in prayer.

Do you see how powerful—yet absolutely simple—the Holy Spirit's leadings and voice can come to us when we're primed and "in shape" because we've been following the Holy Spirit via the Ephesians prayer? My, my, my but He is truly the Greater One who *makes us* a witness. When we are "tuned in" in this way, we don't have to *try* to be a witness, we just are. The voice of the Holy Spirit will be as near and as real to us as our own heartbeat and breath.

Frankly, this is why Christians miss the leading of the Holy Spirit so many times. We are looking to be led like some great evangelist we have heard about. We think we must have a stadium full of people or be called to Africa in order to truly be a witness. But, not true. Every day we can hear the Spirit's voice. Every day He gives us precious promptings **so seemingly common that we mistake them for our own thoughts and emotions.** No, dear one. Since you have been abiding in Him, and He is abiding in you, those things you sense and desire **are** Him leading through you. You really know Him so well!

CHAPTER **14**

FOLLOWING THE INWARD
WITNESS IN **DAILY LIFE**

The sweet faithfulness of the Holy Spirit will speak to you and help you from the smallest issue to the greatest. The same Spirit who has been faithful to lead you through the Word and in prayer is the same Spirit who will lead you in every affair of life.

It's so important that we follow Him every day because in following the same Spirit through the Word, through prayer and through our daily dealings, His voice becomes amplified, defined and confirmed. It will be as though the volume is turned up in our ability to hear. *Then this daily adventure of following Him will line us up at the crossroads of decision to hear His voice, choose His ways. And thus, we will access His plans, His purposes, His protection and His blessings for our lives.*

I've become so accustomed to the help of the Holy Spirit in my everyday life that He's blended into my daily thoughts and ways of doing things. Way back in the beginning of my walk with the Lord, my pastor taught me that if I would spend time in the Bible and prayer, God's daily leadings would become clear to me. He told me that I would become more sensitive to the inward witness of the Holy Ghost, and it's so true. From that time on, I have always endeavored to keep my heart sharp and ready to be guided by Him.

It's funny but I've become so used to His leadings, and they are so much a part of me, that sometimes I no longer make a mental note of it happening. I don't stop in the middle of the sidewalk and say out loud, "Ah ha, the Holy Spirit of the Lord Jesus Christ has just prompted me. I believe I am to head thusly and forthwith into this place or that."

Actually, the number one way the Holy Spirit leads is through the inward witness, and many times it will even be an "unconscious" leading. In reality, you'll get so used to being led and guided by Him that you won't be able to tell the difference between Him and you.

For instance, maybe you'll just suddenly want to go into a store. Or, you'll keep thinking about that girl you need to witness to at the salon. Perhaps you'll keep feeling funny or uncomfortable about taking your vacation on the dates you already requested. Maybe you'll keep being conscious of the tires on your car—because maybe you should head on down to the service station to have them checked out.

Maybe you'll be interviewing someone for a position, but realize even though everything looks amazing on his or her resume that something just is not right. Maybe you'll wonder if you should get more eggs while at the grocery store. Yet, you think, *Nah, I'll get 'em next trip.* Then you arrive home only to discover how right you were since there were already three dozen eggs in the fridge.

These are real and true and not at all religious examples of how the Holy Ghost leads. They are by no means all the ways He leads because He leads and guides in hundreds of ways every single day. These examples are, however, fun, day-to-day illustrations of the variety of ways He can lead you and me.

FINDING CAR KEYS

When I was blonde, finding my car keys was probably one of the greatest ways the Holy Spirit helped me. Actually, it still is! Yes, I praise Jesus that the Holy Spirit helps me to learn scriptures and learn through the avenue of prayer. But, dear me, if I can't find my car keys, I can't go anywhere to help anyone.

So when my car keys seem lost (which happens on a relatively frequent basis for those who are wondering), I will say, "Father God, I'm asking You to help me to find my car keys." I talk to that unction, to the Holy Ghost, asking, "Where are those keys, Lord?" Then I start looking—after all, you must do something, so act on your faith. No, I don't just lie on my bed and wait for the keys to come floating through the air. Listen, the Holy Spirit is not your butler; He is your Helper.

So I ask Him where my keys are and get off my blessed assurance so He can help me find them. As I hunt and root around, I suddenly think of a place: *Yes, hmmm, the kitchen!* But as I head for the kitchen, a sudden knowing and a slight dread fills me. I turn and head for the front door. Ah ha! There they are dangling and stuck in the keyhole of the front door! Yeah, that's right. There they are —right out in front of God and everybody. I just thank God that nobody took them!

AN IMPORTANT MEETING

I had an important meeting with a woman whom I'd heard much about. She was a great woman of ministry and maintained such a strong relationship with the Lord. I was nervous. (OK, you wonder, *You're a Christian, and this lady is a Christian so how could you get nervous?* I know. But guess what? I was still nervous.)

The Holy Ghost helped me as usual and reminded me of a scripture that helped a lot: Psalms 5:12, "For you O Lord will bless the righteous, with favor. You will surround him as with a shield." I also prayed another scripture, Ephesians 6:19, " ... that utterance would be given me." This scripture gives the Lord a place to speak through you with wisdom and revelation. So I asked for favor with this lady and that utterance would be given to me with her.

More than anything, I prayed the prayer found in Ephesians 1:17-23. But coming up close in second place was the combination of Psalms 5:12 for favor and Ephesians 6:19 for utterance. I pray for favor and utterance anytime I am addressing my pastor. I even encourage wives to pray these two scriptures over themselves before they greet their husbands every morning. You would be amazed at the things that come out of your mouth and even more amazed at the things that *don't.*

Ultimately, I went to meet this dear lady at a restaurant. As we sat and talked, I began to see the amazing dialogue of the Holy Ghost and His "strategy" for giving me favor with her. In the midst of our conversation, I found myself making reference time and time again to a minister we both knew. I was amazed at how many times I was referring to this person and how much I knew about this person. I continued to recall story after story about this minister, facts about this minister, insight about this minister. My ears were listening to my own mouth in amazement. After a while, I was more intrigued with what came out of me than even the favor I encountered with this lady.

Finally, I interrupted myself in the midst of a sentence and asked her about the minister we were talking about. "So what's going on here?" I asked. "Do you like this minister a lot or something?" The woman began to laugh. (Actually, right then I blew the whistle on myself. I had prayed for favor and utterance before I went to meet the woman and favor was showing up.)

I finished my question by saying, "I asked you because I find myself talking about this other minister like I am one of those historians on A&E or the Food Network." (What is up with that anyway? Those networks have the hamburger historian, sock historian, Leif Garrett biographer and on and on. Can you believe that people make actual livings doing that and so much so that they have a title?)

This lady went on to tell me that the minister I continued to bring up was, in fact, the person who really "mentored" her for ministry. This minister had impacted her life in a way that no one else had. She had fashioned her own ministry after this person and to this day regards that minister in the highest of esteem. WOW! You see the Holy Spirit wanted us to have fellowship, and He knows how to help people flow together. In fact, He knows how to infuse mutual blessing and ultimately foster divine connections that will last forever.

FAVOR EVERYWHERE YOU GO

Trust me, the Holy Spirit will give you favor everywhere you go. He'll give you favor and utterance with your boss. He'll give you favor and utterance with your husband, your wife—even your teenagers. Now, there's a good one. Try that one out! You'll see some dramatic demonstrations there too! And the Holy Spirit will give you favor and utterance with everyone you contact. Even more, miracle of miracles, the greatest leading of the Holy Spirit may not be for utterance at all—it may be for you to *shut up!*

The best thing you can do for your family and loved ones is simply *to know that if you're related to them, they probably will not receive anything you try to preach because they're too familiar with you.* Sometimes the best thing you can do regarding your family is to proclaim Acts 16:31, where Paul told the Philippian jailer, "Believe on the Lord Jesus Christ, and you will be saved, you and your *household.*" Proclaim it to the Lord in the place of prayer, remind Him that you are trusting Him for this blessed promise. Instead of running your mouth to your family—run your mouth to the Lord and let *Him* find a way into their hearts. You might just be in the way! After all, your loved ones are your inheritance.

Boldly proclaim while driving your car or mowing the lawn, "Father, no matter what it looks like or feels like, I thank You that my kids are saved, filled with the Holy Ghost and serving God." "Father, I thank You that my dad and mom are saved and going to heaven." "Father, I thank You that my husband is on fire and serving God, and I vow not to nag him." "Father, I thank You that my wife and mother of my children is a born-again Christian and following you."

Boldly proclaim salvation over your family and loved ones on a daily basis, especially when it looks the worst. Especially decree it when they are appearing to be the *exact opposite of what you're believing* for in prayer. Then pray the prayer found in Matthew 9:38, "...pray the Lord of the harvest to send laborers into His fields...." God will begin to send laborers across their paths. You watch how quickly your loved ones come in as you pray and proclaim these things.

If you will let Him, the Holy Spirit will help you to prosper in your daily work life. He will teach you to prosper (Isaiah 48:17). He will use your time in the workplace to actually form and fashion you for what you are called to do. If you will prove faithful, the Holy Spirit will promote you and cause favor to come upon your work. He will give you solutions to problems that have haunted your company and industry for years. He will give you wisdom beyond your years and benefits beyond your tenure. He will do for you as He did for Abraham, He will bless you so you may become a blessing.

A FAITHFUL FRIEND RECEIVES HELP FROM 'THE HELPER'

I met a dear friend of mine at a church women's meeting. We shall call her Dee. Actually, so many women attended that the church had to utilize the men's restrooms for the women as well. In order to make the men's restrooms a little more "feminine friendly," they put flower arrangements in the urinals. (There's a mental picture for you.) It was in this most memorable setting I met Dee. She helped me fasten my necklace.

Yet, it wasn't long before long our paths crossed again as we both began volunteering at a ministry in Tulsa. I remembered her the moment I saw her. I volunteered to clean, and Dee volunteered to do clerical work. Actually, Dee had studied to be a dental hygienist, but in following her heart and being guided by the Holy Ghost she began doing clerical work for the ministry.

Dee was so faithful. She would pray over her work all the time and did not endeavor to perform her duties simply with her natural abilities. She would pray asking the Lord to help her to work as unto the Lord. She asked for favor and ability to help as she ought and asked the Holy Spirit "to make her a blessing" to this ministry. She was a wonderful help. Dee was a great example of following the Helper, the Holy Spirit.

Meanwhile, I had been thinking about the head of the ministry. In my prayer times it seemed that the Holy Spirit would bring him up to me and remind me that he had books in his heart he wanted to do. I began to wonder why those books had not been written yet so one day when I was talking to him I asked about the books. He explained that he did not want to write the books himself. He wanted someone to listen to the CDs of his preaching, type everything up, and then edit the writings into book form.

"I need an editor," he said. "If I could only find an editor who would catch the heart of what I am wanting."

Wow, I thought, *We all had better start praying for an editor for him.*

Meanwhile, the ministry needed catchphrases for some CD covers. For lack of anyone else available, they asked the office staff if they could come up with something. Dee would always come through. Any article or correspondence she did would always reflect the heart of the ministry. She never took anything for granted; she never approached anything in her own strength or abilities. Dee would always enlist the help of the Helper.

Dee would always look to the Lord to help her, guide her, teach her and inspire her to really be a *help to* this ministry. Only the Helper, the Holy Spirit, can empower a person to truly *help* another. She would not seek her own ways of doing things, but continually submitted herself to the help of the Holy Spirit. In doing so, He was *making* her to be a blessing. In fact, it wasn't long before the head of the ministry came to Dee with the tapes and CDs and asked her to put them in book form. They also hired Dee and brought her on full time.

Now, catch the reality of this. Dee was a dental hygienist who had no formal editing training. She had not been to college for journalism or creative writing. Dee was just faithful day after day, allowing the Holy Spirit to train her as He would have her help. *Yet, her faithfulness began to chisel out God's plan for her.*

Dee took those tapes and CDs and laid them

before the Lord. She laid herself before the Lord, a living sacrifice as it were. She told the Lord she could only do this work if the Holy Spirit helped her. It reminded me of how Moses argued with God. You'll recall that God trained Moses on the backside of the desert, tending sheep. Then at the right time, God instructed Moses to shepherd a new flock—the people of Israel.

Frustrated in what he perceived as his inability, Moses responded to the Lord, saying, "Oh Lord, I cannot speak. I am not eloquent."

"Who do you think makes mouths?" God essentially responded to Moses.

Then the Lord said a funny thing to Moses. He said, "I will be with your mouth."

If you will let Him, God also will be with your mouth as you speak on a daily basis. God will be with your pen, your computer, your wrench, your presentation— whatever tool is needed—if you will let Him. He will bless you and then make you a blessing. He'll do it if you will only pray: God give me favor; God give me utterance; God help me to help.

And so Dee prayed. And so Dee began to write. The book began to form and even began to fly out! And so the book unfolded. It was a portrait of the minister who preached it and was prepared as though the minister had penned it himself. Dee had communicated the exact inflections, the perfect transitions. She had caught the spirit of what was to be said. **She had come to understand by the Holy Ghost the heart of the ministry and the spirit of what needed to be communicated.** All the while, Dee's heart was so pure; her motive only to do God's will and to be a blessing. This is why the Lord could use her. She was teachable, pliable and filled with faith in the Lord's faithfulness.

In fact, Dee's faithfulness taught me a great lesson. You see, a few years later, the Lord began to prompt Dee about a change coming. The same voice, the same inward witness, the same Spirit whom she had yielded to in order to help that ministry began to talk to her of another assignment. That same Helper, the Holy Ghost, revealed to her that God's will for her was for her to begin her own publishing company. Amazing, isn't it?

Actually, it's like the format we see in Acts 13. There we see that the apostle Paul gets placed into the ministry God has called him to (verse 2). Even though Paul was a foundational apostle and wrote two-thirds of the New Testament, he still had to be separated into the ministry God had for him. Paul had been a preacher and a teacher for at least 13 years, but it was not until Acts 13 that he was finally separated unto the ministry where the Lord had actually called him. Paul had phenomenal gifting and wow what a call! Yet, it was neither the call nor the gifting that finally separated him unto the actual ministry God had for him—it was *faithfulness*.

Paul said so himself. In 1 Timothy 1:12 he says, "I thank Christ Jesus our Lord...because He *counted me faithful*, putting me into the ministry." It was faithfulness to follow the inward witness of the Holy Spirit that ultimately positioned him in the ministry where God had called him. Want more proof? Acts 13:2 says, "The *Holy Spirit said*, now separate Barnabas and Saul *unto me for the work whereunto I have called them."* Paul had been *faithful* to the Holy Spirit, and it was that same Holy Spirit who then separated Paul unto the same ministry whereunto the same Holy Spirit had called him. Hallelujah!

Luke 16:10 and 12 share astounding truths with us. "He who is faithful in what is least is faithful also in much." Verse 12 goes on to tell us, *"If you have not been faithful in what is another man's, who will give you what is your own?"* You see Dee followed the Helper or Holy Spirit so well that He was able to fine-tune, test and train her. Through the power of the Holy Ghost, Jesus was able to *make* her a blessing. Because Dee learned to yield to the Helper, Jesus was able to place her into her ultimate call.

You see, the Holy Spirit is ultimately called to help the believer bring about the calling of the Lord Jesus on the earth. Jesus is coming back for a bride—for a *helpmeet.* That's right—He's coming back for a fully grown, mature helper and co-laborer. How can you be sure that you're ready to take your place? Yielding to the Holy Spirit in your daily life—on the job and with family and friends—will form and fashion you for your calling on the earth and ultimately prepare you to meet the One you will *help* forever.

What a blessed truth this is. What a pathway of blessing for those who will dare to find and follow that invisible map. *You* know that map. *You* know that way. *You* know that voice.

CHAPTER 15

REAL-LIFE LEADINGS OF GOD

Truth be told, I'm a little nervous writing about how I've been led by the inward witness regarding finances because I'm a preacher. I explained to the Lord that I didn't want to share how I—the preacher— have been led because my goal is to reach businessmen, laborers, waitresses, doctors and folks who hold down more regular jobs.

But the Lord quickened to me that regarding finances and the prosperity of the Lord that everyone has to follow the same inward witness in order to tap into the prosperity or economy of the Lord. After all, the preacher does not live by preaching; the preacher—like every Christian—*must live by faith.* In fact, Romans 1:17 says, "The just shall live by faith." And so the pattern of following the Holy Ghost into prosperity is the same for all.

I have many testimonies of being led further and further into financial prosperity, but this particular testimony of His gracious leading stands out. As an itinerant or traveling minister, there have been certain times that meetings were kind of, how shall I say it? They were staying away in droves. Yes, that captures it. However, I quickly learned that even if the meetings were staying away, the expenses of daily living kept coming in anyway.

In all honesty, that's when "calling pastors fever" kicks in. Trying to find phone numbers of pastors who might have me in their churches to speak and feeling the pressure of finances breathing down my neck. Wow—that's like a great way to make calls, isn't it? Talk about doubt and unbelief.

The truth is, faith puts no pressure on people for people are not our source. Even our jobs are not our final source. Whether in a job or in our dealings with people, the economy of our Father God wants to invade our job setting, our attitudes, our ideas, our limitations and ultimately our bank accounts. So I backed off and got back to the Father God on the whole topic of prosperity. I prayed the Ephesians prayer over and over and began to read about prosperity in my Bible. At first I read in a kind of a dutiful sweating fashion. My eyes looked at the pages, but my mind was frantic and my heart was racing. *What am I gonna do? What am I gonna do? What am I gonna do?* I wondered.

In blind faith I kept reading my Bible under the influence of the Ephesians prayer. I had prayed the Ephesians prayer, that is Ephesians 1:17-23, with regard to prosperity. Whooops! Sure enough, scriptures began to be highlighted to me. "Wow!" I would say. "This scripture is awesome, but what am I gonna do?" I made myself write down that scripture, and then I'd keep on reading. Before I knew it, the power of the Ephesians prayer and the Holy Spirit had divinely sidetracked me from my doubts and fears. The Helper had downloaded faith into my heart—so much so that it blasted doubt and fear out of my head. The answer became so clear in my heart. It was like—*ding!* "You've got mail!"

Here's the simple—yet profound—step I took next: **I worshipped the Lord with the very truths the Holy Spirit had enlightened to me.**

Powerful and vital instructions for life are right here. When the Spirit of God gives you a scripture, dare to **worship** the Lord with that **truth**. Have you ever done this? Have you ever worshipped the Father with a truth? I know in the modern church today there is so much worship—worship CDs, worship seminars, worship leaders, worship services. There's worship, worship, worship. All the worship is wonderful and of the utmost importance. *But,* have you ever turned off the worship CD for just a little while and *dared to worship the Lord with a truth from His Word?* I am not even talking about singing. I am talking about speaking God's word back to Him in an attitude of worship—worshipp9ing Him with a promise like it has already happened.

John 4:23 says that God is seeking someone— anyone—who might worship Him with a truth. What do you mean? How do you mean?

Simply take the truth or truths the Holy Spirit has highlighted to you and with definite purpose—no matter what you feel or how bad circumstances look—begin to worship God with the *truth* of a given situation. ***Take the scriptures that the powerful Ephesians prayer has "made alive" to you and "sacrifice" them back to God.*** With the fruit of your lips a living sacrifice, take scriptures and begin to thank God for the reality of them in your life. This may feel like the ultimate sacrifice because things and people—even your own doubts and fears—make it seem impossible to worship Him or magnify this scripture as true in your situation. **But that is where your sacrifice—your true worship—comes into play.**

"I will magnify the Lord, O my soul, I will forget none of His benefits" (Psalm 103:2). Begin to say from your heart, "Yes, Lord, You have exalted the name of Jesus above every name. God, You have exalted Your Word even above Your own name. So, God, if You exalt Your Word that high—above every circumstance, shortcoming, weakness, sin, offense and impossibility—then I follow Your example. I will do no less. Right now, no matter what I feel like, no matter what the situation looks like, I exalt Your Word. I worship You with Your truth. I repeat back to You that which You have spoken to me."

I worshipped the Lord with the scriptures He had given me. I began with Galatians 3:13, which reminds Christians they are "blessed with believing Abraham." In Genesis 13:2, it says "Abram [God later changed his name to Abraham.] was very rich in gold, in silver, in cattle and livestock...." It goes on to say "Abram was blessed to be a blessing."

Further, in Genesis 14:18–23, we see a portrait of Abram as a generous giver. We also see him lifting his hand and vowing it would never be said that any man had made him rich. Abram purposed to follow God in such a way that his "profiting would be evident to all." Abram was an example of someone who followed after God. He sought first God's kingdom and God's path to prosperity so it would be heralded that God made Abram rich. Abram purposed to be a testimony, a billboard, a divine advertisement of the provision and goodness and abundance of God. As a result, Abram demonstrated the loving true character of

God. Abram was a foretaste of the limitless Giver who would give us Jesus. Hallelujah!

So I took these scriptures and thanked the Lord that according to His Word, the highest authority in the universe, that my God was supplying all my need according to His riches in Christ Jesus no matter what the circumstances looked like or felt like. I thanked Him that my husband and I were blessed with Abraham because we believed God and we are in Christ. I worshipped the Father and reminded Him of His Word. (As you can plainly see, I reminded myself too. I magnified the Lord until He looked big to me too!) I reminded Him over and over, and I reminded myself over and over, that He is my source and that no man supplies my need.

Then the Holy Ghost brought more scriptures to my remembrance. The great inward witness of my abundant supply from heaven began to abound in my heart. My faith began to soar, and thus, grace and peace began to come upon me—a grace that frightens away fears. A grace came by which I could serve Him acceptably, a grace that caused me to labor more abundantly. A grace came to believe, to trust and to escape the snare of worry and panic. A grace came to escape just plain wrong leadings.

I've found that as you worship the Lord with the scriptures, the Holy Ghost supplies you with a grace that will begin to **manifest**. So I began to speak edification and comfort to myself. I began to speak that my husband and I together would become like a mighty river with regard to teaching on the subject of united prayer. As I continued to pray, I saw that wherever the river went, people would be washed from their sins, their thirst would be quenched, and ultimately, the river would dump into the sea where the fishing would be great. In other words, we'd be able to reach people who don't know the Lord. (There is a scripture of this very scenario in Ezekiel 47. Imagine that, the Holy Spirit breaking open a scriptural passage and making it seem as though my husband and I were right in the middle of it.)

Then the Holy Ghost broke open **a thought** to me the same way the scriptures broke open to me. Yes, a strong, encouraging, and almost atomic-filled blessing filled my mind. It was this: "You know, all along the river **there are banks!** I began to laugh and shout. Woo hoo! Yeah! Amen.

Banks! *You know, those places that hold lots and lots and lots money.* **Banks! Yeah, banks!**

Friend, if we just remain in the river of the Lord, the banks—the Source, God Almighty Himself—shall supply all our needs according to *His riches in glory!* Hallelujah! How do we stay in the river? John 7:38 says, "out of your belly will flow *rivers....*" *Whoa!*

I was encouraged; I could feel a **tangible grace and peace rest upon me and rise up within me.** My circumstances outwardly had not changed, and my bank account looked none the friendlier. However, **I had changed**, and make no mistake, my source had changed too. Now the Holy Ghost had arisen and born faith in my heart. Now the inward witness was strong and loud and ready to lead me into the prosperity of my Savior.

Proverbs 10:22 says of this prosperity: "The blessing of the Lord maketh truly rich, and it adds no sorrow." Actually, that verse goes on to say that "neither does toiling increase it!" Did you know that you can have tons of money and never have peace or joy or the strength of God in your bones to enjoy it? Did you know that you can work long hours and long days and never enter into the wealth of spirit, soul and body that only the Savior can bestow?

"Thy will be done on earth as it is in heaven." Jesus prayed. There is no poverty in heaven. It is a city made of absolute gold and wealth, and there's no sorrow in the place. There are no ulcers, no worry about an economy that could collapse or shift suddenly. It's the place of true riches.

With all this peace and joy in my heart, what do you think I immediately did? Run and call a pastor? No! I called some other people I knew just to talk and fellowship and minister to them. Why not? Since the Lord is taking care of us, we're free to minister to others.

Also, I felt led to send an offering to a specific ministry. *What, you wonder, I thought you needed finances?* Well, my God supplies all my needs and the Holy Ghost prompted me to send an offering to another minister. Do you know what happen next? Pastors began to call me. People began to send us offerings. Even greater, a leading and a witness from the Holy Ghost came regarding direction—what church to go to next, what state to go to next. We received further revelation regarding "doors of ministry" opening to us and ministerial opportunities we should accept.

Friend, let me tell you. This is not a one-time testimony; this has become my lifestyle. It can become yours too. As you worship the Lord with a scripture the Holy Spirit has given you, a grace will manifest upon and even around your person and life.

Paul the apostle said in Galatians 2:9, "When James, Cephas, and John, who seemed to be pillars, **perceived the grace** that had been given to me, they gave me and Barnabas the right hand of fellowship...." How true. When you worship the Father with a truth by the Spirit, God's grace in that area is manifested and people and even situations **perceive that grace**. Then that grace will open doors of opportunity, ideas, connections and favor. Favor! **Favor!** Oh, the unmerited favor of God! Great favor! People just want to hire you; people just want to listen to you. Because of favor ideas come to you! You work better; you work as unto God! You're irresistible—all because of God's grace.

Second Corinthians 9:8 in The Amplified Bible says the following, "God is able to make all grace (every favor and earthly blessing) come to you in abundance, so that you may always and under all circumstances and whatever the need be self-sufficient...furnished in abundance for every good work." That scripture shows us the pattern of faith. Here it is laid out once again. We worship the Lord with the truths the Holy Spirit highlights to us; then the grace of God comes upon us.

That grace will be perceived even by "situations," if you will. Situations regarding finance will favor you. People will favor you. Doors of favor will open to you. And then, in context with the previously mentioned scripture, **earthly blessing will come to you in abundance.**

Let's get real. There's no substance more earthly than money, gold or cold hard cash. Earthly blessings are things like houses, lands, properties, investments, cars and customers. Earthly blessings are things like college tuition for your children and airplane tickets to travel to nations with the gospel. Also the very context of 2 Corinthians 9:8 especially in The Amplified Bible is couched within an entire passage dealing with finances.

You can count on the inward witness of the Holy Spirit to lead you to the right opportunities. He will give you financial ideas. If you work for a corporation, He will teach you how to do your job with excellence until you rise to the very top. He will prompt you in such a way that you become a blessing to your employer, the employees and the entire business. The company will be blessed because you are there. If the Lord wants to create a new venue for you, He could even inspire you to start a business. If He does, He will give you the idea, the plan, the purpose and the pursuit of it. He will supply you with ability and know how. He will even give you the "the want to" to get it going. When God inspires you to do a business, it will bless you and bless other people as well. The blessing will just never stop.

You will be led by the very source of all blessings, the Holy Ghost Himself. He has treasures for you in heavenly places of fellowship as you worship Him in the spirit with a truth. He will free you from the love of money so you're free to love God and follow God. You can go and do whatever He tells you to do. And wherever He tells you to go, He'll be your source and your supply. You will no longer serve mammon, but you will serve God. *You are free to serve God, and thus, money will now serve you.* Hallelujah!

One Weird Wart

There's pretty much no end to the goodness of God. Just as you learn to worship God with regard to prosperity, you can worship God right straight into healing for your body. I'll prove it to you with the story of one weird wart.

This ugly wart showed up on my hand. I could have put wart medicine on it, and I planned on going to the doctor to get it removed. That would have been easy and done away with the thing. However, the Lord dealt with me about trusting Him to rid me of it. He dealt with me that the same victory and faith that would overcome that wart, would help me to help other people to overcome sickness and disease. After all, it's all the same faith. So I decided I would just worship the wart away.

Now, let me make one thing really clear. Doctors are awesome. Never think it is doubt to go to a doctor. If you're afraid to go to a doctor, you probably are not in faith anyway. Doctors are good. Healing is good. Get annual checkups. Get tests. Get health insurance. Don't move in presumption; move in faith.

Get this now: Doctor, **good**; not going to doctor, **bad**. Me Tarzan. You Jane. Monkey. Banana.

OK, all that said, I settled in to worship God regarding the wart. I decided that I might as well do this faith project now so I'd be ready should any other physical test show up. So I prayed the Ephesians prayer, which ushered me straight into the so called *"New Testament clinic."* After praying the Ephesians prayer with regard to healing, I was drawn again to Galatians 3:13, which says, **"Christ hath redeemed us from the curse of the law, being made a curse for us..." (KJV).** Therefore, if we're redeemed from the "curse of the law," I better head to the Old Testament to find out exactly what the "curse of the law" is so I can see what I was redeemed from.

A list of all the "curses" is found in Deuteronomy 28. The list names all the "curses" that would come upon the children of Israel if they did not obey the Ten Commandments. This is also why it's so important to enter the Old Testament through the "slant" or "interpretation" of the New Testament. You see, Galatians 3:13 tells the New Testament saint that he or she is redeemed or delivered from the curse of breaking the law of the Old Testament. Christ is the fulfillment of the law to all who believe according to Romans 10:4. That's great news for us! We can read those curses knowing we're free from them.

Awesome! That horrendous list of curses has become a divine menu of blessings so I can see what can no longer haunt or vex me. It's a lavish list of redemption. Item by item I see that the blood of Jesus has vanquished the enemy and turned his fear-filled dominating atrocities into a victorious and liberating catalog of ironies. In other words, if Deuteronomy 28 lists something as a curse, then according to Galatians 3 it has become a blessing to me. I am willing; I am obedient by the power of the Lord Jesus Christ. Therefore, these curses are turned into blessings headed my way.

Please go read the listings in Deuteronomy 28 to find out what you are redeemed from; you will see the list has many references to healing. The real kicker is that even if you don't find an exact affliction listed there, verse 61 takes care of that too. It takes care of all the leftovers and says, "Also **every sickness**, and **every plague**, which is not written in the book of this law, them will the Lord bring upon thee, until thou be destroyed," (verse 61). That means if you have a sickness, disease or symptom that is "new" or not listed, it does not matter. The Word of God plainly states that every sickness, plague and disease is a part of the curse. Therefore, you're redeemed from it, and it has no right to dwell in your body.

Deuteronomy 28 lists quite a lot of amazing things you are redeemed from. Things like confusion, vexation of heart, your children leaving you, poverty, even working and all your money some how slipping away no matter how hard you work. Awesome!

You are redeemed!

So I was led to Deuteronomy 28:27 in the New King James Version, "The Lord will strike you with the boils of Egypt, with tumors...." When I looked up the word tumor in Webster's Dictionary, it meant "an abnormal benign new growth of tissue that possesses no physiological function and arises from uncontrolled usually rapid cellular proliferation." That sounds wartlike enough for me. Another dictionary said "any kind of tissue growth that differs from the surrounding tissue." Yep—again, sounds like Mr. Wart and his job description. Mr. Wart is about to get fired!

I took my truths that the Holy Spirit had rooted out via the Ephesians prayer, and I began to worship God with them. I thanked the Lord that according to Galatians 3:13 that I am redeemed from the curse of the law. I thanked Him that according to Galatians

3:13 part of the curse was tumors and growths, and I'm redeemed from that. I thanked Him that His flesh was ripped open so that my skin might remain blameless, untainted, without blemish or spot.

I worshipped God with uplifted hands yet never looking at my hands. I did not worship Him all the while looking at that wart to see if it had changed. I worshipped Him until **peace and joy** came into my heart and flooded my mind, will and emotions.

Dear friend, your answer is not the manifestation of that for which you believe. Your answer is peace and joy arising in your heart. That *is* faith! **In fact, it's the evidence of joy and peace that let's you know you are believing and trusting God!** Faith is now; joy and peace are now, and these are the "fuel tank readings" that show you are full and on the way to your manifestation. Worship until joy and peace flood your heart.

If we will worship with a truth in the spirit, then we will see naturally that silly little "after effect" of the manifestation in the natural. The natural is but temporal and must bow to the substance of faith that framed the worlds and frames our victory. Woo hoo!

Needless to say, I got blessed worshipping. I got, as they say in California, "just like sooo blessed—that's like nuclear awesome!" Then I went off to work.

At that time, I was working as a waitress, which made life interesting. Did you know that when you serve people their food, they look at your hands? Yup, they do. Clean healthy hands are like kind of important when handling people's meals. That's not to mention there's like an entire governmental department about it—so called the health department. They're the people who keep the hairnet companies in business despite the fact that the 1950s style has come and gone. Needless to say—when I would set people's plates down, they would see this wart that would like wave at them and introduce itself. It most certainly did not enhance the waitressing experience. Aside from the pain and discomfort this wart caused, it made me feel insecure. Sickness is mean. Infirmity doesn't play fair.

The funny thing is that as soon as I began to worship the Lord about my healing, *that stupid wart got even bigger.* What? Yeah. I mean it got **huge!** How could that happen?

Well, here's a funk-o-rama scripture. Mark 4:15 says, "Satan comes immediately to take away the Word that was sown in their hearts." The devil like so does not want you to get a victory in the area of healing. He knows that all you need is one manifested victory, and then the same faith lesson will be practiced over and over again on any sickness, disease or plague. He knows you'll then become a witness and a testimony to the power and goodness of God. Yikes—he can't have that! So sometimes when you begin to stand for healing, the symptoms actually get worse. *But—**hold your ground!***

So the wart got bigger. Then it got bigger still. Eventually it obtained its own ZIP code. It developed a gravitational pull, and thus, its own moons—two or three of them, NASA reported. It became so big I began to drag my hand on the ground like an enormous baboon. Small clusters of squirrels came to live near it as it became a mountain with its own heat source. The EPA even contacted me as they saw it could be a source of heat energy. And, in fact, it was later defined as an undetected fault line, which opened and produced seismic waves of lava. Had Google Earth been in existence, you probably could have seen it on an iPhone app. I am saying it was HUGE! And it got worse again.

Then the thing cracked open and started oozing some kind of clear goop, which looked like mayonnaise. Make note to self: When you serve food, people only want mayonnaise on their sandwich—not dripping from a waitress's finger like typhoid Rita. Customers ran out of the restaurant in terror; small children developed stuttering problems at the sight of it. The wart began to wear a bandanna. It got a tattoo. It joined a gang. It would taunt me all the time and threaten to overtake my entire visage. I think it even got up one night and moved my furniture around. It was mean.

That wart got so big that it began to fascinate me. It was as though the inward witness or revelation of the Holy Ghost was showing me that this was the ridiculously "overplayed hand" of the enemy. The rapid change in its growth and "gross factor" kind of stood out to me, intrigued me and provoked me to the point that it became *obvious to me that this was the devil.* As soon as I had begun to worship the Lord with a truth, that wart seemed to get mad and boast, "Well, I'll show her!" The devil had just thrown a small growth at me at the beginning, but then this lying symptom grew bigger and bigger. It's daunting size and characteristics seem to brag and taunt me. It's as though the state of these symptoms were trying to intimidate my faith.

At first it was only a small nuisance, but then all of

the sudden it was like the devil threw the kitchen sink at me. Well, let me tell you. The Holy Ghost rose up on the inside of me with a righteous indignation and a boldness that is not my own. I proclaimed, "That's it!" I don't care how big this stupid wart gets, I don't care if it joins a political party and runs for president. I am redeemed from this growth, and it has to go! The peace and joy of the Holy Ghost enveloped me.

Actually, the powerful inward witness of the Spirit rose up so strongly in me, that I began to laugh. I laughed and laughed and laughed. I laughed not only with peace, but also with joy so strong that it couldn't be contained in words. I had to laugh. I laughed at the absurdity of that stupid wart. The Holy Ghost showed me how silly and outlandishly obvious the plans of the enemy were. Man what a joke!

Dude, you may need to laugh at a few of your circumstances or symptoms. Laugh! When you move into laughing at what the enemy has tried, your captivity will be turned! Faith-filled laughter is an access or gateway to blessings that are in heavenly places. He who sits in the heavens laughs!

The Bible says, "When the Lord turned the captivity of Zion, we were as those that dream! Then our mouth was filled with laughter" (Psalm 126:1-2). In the presence of the Lord there is a fullness of joy (Psalm 16:11). Dude! Dancing on the devil's head is fun. You may even sense a laugh rising up right now! Take it! When you move over into laughing about your situation—whatever it may be—again, that's where the greatest blessings in the Lord begin to manifest. Then, God will turn your whole life around. Glory! That's how we learn the ways of the Holy Ghost, and then He's free to quicken our mortal bodies in the same way He raised Jesus from the dead. What an awesome, nuclear, totally rad blessing!

One morning about a week later, I woke up and just as suddenly and surprisingly as that wart had exploded into a mountain, that wart suddenly—but not surprisingly—was no longer there. Poof! It was gone! Cast into the sea of forgetfulness if you ask me. No mark, no scar, no trace. My skin had no "remembrance" that it had ever existed. Another mountain cast into the sea by faith. Hallelujah!

HOLY GHOST HELP WITH RELATIONSHIPS

When I was 21 years old, I became a Christian. My family thought I was insane and had joined a cult. I suppose that was supported in part by the fact that I began to frantically witness to my mom, my dad and my sister as most new Christians do. I put tracks in their mailbox. I nagged. I threatened. I cried and begged. I tried over and over to explain. But the more I pestered them, the further away they went.

A wise minister once said, "Never try to witness to your own family. They won't listen to you just because *you are family*; they're overly familiar with you. Instead, pray Matthew 9:38 over them and trust the Lord to send laborers across their pathway." So I began to pray that prayer for them. (Well, actually, I still kind of nagged them. I mean, after all, I knew God's will for them, right? But again, the more I bugged them the further they went.)

Once again, I turned to the power of the Ephesians prayer. The "great-all-purpose-will-of-God-finder" prayer as I call it. Again, attach it wherever you need revelation. Attach it to a nation to learn how to reap that nation by revelation. Attach it to a ministry, attach it to finances, attach it to healing for a revelation of how healed you really are. Or, pray it with regard to a family member and watch the Lord walk you through to victory in that relationship.

Once again I flung open my Bible to pray the Ephesians prayer and then started reading scriptures throughout the New Testament. The Holy Ghost brought to my remembrance a scripture passage in Acts 16:29-31, where the apostle Paul spoke some important words to a newly saved convert. God sent a miracle to rescue Paul who was in jail. The jail cell popped open, and the Philippian jailer got saved because of it. Then Paul gave a mighty promise to this guard **regarding his family**, saying, "Believe on the Lord Jesus Christ and you will be saved, you and **your entire household!**" Wow! That's awesome! **We're also given a promise for our entire family.**

Then as I was reading the Gospels through the lenses of the Ephesians prayer, another passage of scripture seemed to speak as though in stereo. Matthew 6 says, "Seek ye first the kingdom of God and his righteousness, and all these *things* that the world seeks will be added to you." Now I know this sounds funny, but the Holy Spirit reminded me that Proverbs 18:22 says, "He that finds a wife finds a *good thing* and obtains favor from the Lord." So, if a wife can be a *thing*, then a husband can be a *thing*, a brother or sister can be a *thing*, a mom or dad can be a *thing* and so on.

Right then I made a decision in my heart. As an act of faith, I purposed to seek first the kingdom of

God; I purposed to passionately seek the Lord. I decided if I ever become discouraged because I don't see my loved ones saved yet, I'll pursue the plans, purposes and pursuits of my Father even more. In faith I'll be relentless so my dear, precious beloved family *things* shall be added to me.

Then the Holy Spirit took me to a most unusual set of scriptures. As always, I started out in the New Testament—actually, I remain there, camp there and flourish there. Then, all of the sudden, the light and leading of the New Testament catapulted me into the Old Testament, where I found some amazing scriptures. Jeremiah 9:4 says " ...do not trust any brother...." Jeremiah 17:5-8 says, "Cursed is the man who trusts in man and makes flesh his strength ... for he shall be like a shrub in the desert, and shall not see when good comes.... Blessed is the man who trusts in the Lord ... for he shall be like a tree planted by the waters...." That man who trusts in the Lord will flourish.

The Lord gave me a thought, a concept, if you will. He gave me a "way better idea" than Ford or anything I could have thought up. This "idea" or "thought" or "way of looking at things" seemed so much better than any of my ways. It seemed higher, even heavenly. Ready? Here's the idea: **Quit trusting in man; start trusting in God!**

That got me. I should quit trusting in my own ability to nag, condemn, threaten, cry, worry or beg. In essence, I should quit trusting in my own ability to save these people. Jesus is the Savior, and there is no other name by which men or women may be saved. At last, I saw it! My job was simply to put my trust in Jesus that my loved ones would be saved and go on serving God.

I gathered the promises that the Holy Spirit had carved out for me via the chisel of the Ephesians prayer, and I began to worship the Lord with these truths in the spirit. I said, "Lord, I thank You for Your Word, and I thank You there's an answer for every situation in it. Right now, Father, I exalt Your Word above the names even of my family. You are Greater, and You want them to know You and follow You even more than I could ever desire.

"So, I worship You with the truths You've given me, and I purpose in accordance with Matthew 6:33 to consecrate myself and pursue first Your plan, purpose and pursuits. I will passionately follow You and put You first, knowing that according to Matthew 6:33 that You—not me—will cause all my 'things' or family members to come to know You.

"Now, as an act of my will, I purpose to follow hard after You and watch confidently as You perform all You've promised. Also, Father, in accordance with Proverbs 3:5, I actively put my trust in You regarding my family. I do not trust in my own ability, neither do I put trust in my family members to do the right thing. My trust is solidly in You.

"Lord, you said in Acts 16:31, 'Believe on the Lord Jesus Christ, and you will be saved, you and *your household.*' So, my Father, I trust You and worship You with this truth with great thanksgiving no matter what it looks like or feels like. No matter how my family acts, I see them saved and serving You through the eye of faith, dear Lord. Now, I thank You for it and worship You for it!"

Keep in mind, this prayer is not a one-time event. Nope. It's a *lifestyle* of Bible study, prayer and worship that yields fruit time and time again. I would especially kick it up on the worshipping side when my family would start to act contrary to what the scriptures deemed. I would again worship in this way so as to steady my own emotions and seal in my faith with peace and joy. So I continued to worship the Lord with the scriptures the Holy Spirit would give me regarding my family, and I also continued to thank the Lord for laborers to cross their paths.

I continued to believe for my family as time passed. Then, out of the blue one day my sister called to tell me she was pregnant. Honestly, it upset me because I knew she did not know the Lord. However, because my *trust was in the Lord and not in pressuring or nagging her*, my response was a result of my trust in the Lord. I simply said, "Awesome!"

Here's the point. We may love people and actually know what is best for them, but if we nag, beg and condemn them, we'll only drive them further away. The truth is, nagging, begging, condemning, threatening, crying and worry all stem from doubt and unbelief. Bottom line, God doesn't pressure and drive people, and we shouldn't either. If you will allow the Lord to highlight scriptures to you and then worship Him with those scriptures, that grace we've talked about will come upon you and cause you to respond differently to people. As you worship the Lord with these truths and trust Him—not trust in the arm of the flesh—you will literally begin to act differently around those you want to see saved. Your actions will be prompted by the inward witness in directives of love and faith. You will find yourself at peace around the people you're praying for, and you will be able to love them selflessly. They will be drawn to you, and you will win them by your conduct—without a single word.

So while I was on the phone with my sister, I was kind and supportive. Why not? My trust was in the Lord. As I hung up the phone, the Holy Ghost spoke important words to me in a very "authoritative voice." It was not audible with my physical ears, but it was loud and clear just the same. Most of the time, the Holy Spirit communicates through an inward witness, but on this occasion a more "spectacular" manifestation occurred. He said, "That baby will be the key to her salvation!" This promise brought great comfort to me, and that baby's name eventually became Justin. Year after year I held on to these words. I continued to worship God with the truth of His Word, and as promised I continued to pursue the Lord with all my heart.

Then no less than 12 years later, I got a call one day from my sister who excitedly said she'd gotten saved. Awesome! When I asked her what happened, she said that one day Justin came out to where she was gardening and began to talk to her. The now 12-year-old boy simply asked, "Mom, 'Will you please get saved on Sunday so you won't go to hell when you die?' "

"Yes!" she replied to her son.

Whoa. It was that simple!

One day it simply came about because through faith and patience we inherit the promises. As we worship God with truths, the Spirit helps soothe our souls and soak us in the "staying power" of Spirit-authored patience. Listen! There are seasons when big blessings just start popping and showing up—if we don't faint.

In that same phone call from my sister, she said, "Hey, Dana, I got saved, and now I'm taking Mom to church on Sunday so the pastor can save her too!" Sure enough, my mom got saved the following Sunday. Praise God!

Don't get hung up on the just-saved lingo. We know that pastors don't save people; Jesus does. But I so enjoyed the raw excitement of what she said. I also love how the Lord always makes a way. If we put God's Word to work, it will work every time.

It will work for you! Pray the Ephesians prayer, read your Bible and let scriptures become real to you. Then take those scriptures and worship the Lord while following the inward witness of the Holy Ghost. Let Him bear witness to certain actions and words and prompts that will draw your family to Him. Like honey, His Words are sweeter than the honeycomb (Psalm 19:10). These precious truths ministered by the Spirit of God will cause your loved ones to come to know Him all the while transforming you into a great "truster" of God. They will adorn you with a meek and quiet spirit as you manifest the faith, joy and peace of God, which is precious in the sight of God. Glory!

CHAPTER 16

A **LIFESTYLE** OF TRUE WORSHIP

A pattern of "true worship in Spirit and in truth" can be—and should be—applied in your life. In fact, it can become a format to victory in every area of life.

If you feel like you continually fall in an area considered sin, apply this practice of the Word. Exercise yourself unto righteousness. Pray the Ephesians prayer, and read the New Testament. Find scriptures that declare how very righteous you are by the blood of Jesus, and then worship the Father with these truths. Thank Him no matter what you look like or act like because the blood of Jesus is greater than any and every evil tendency.

Magnify the Lord and extol Him according to 2 Corinthians 5:21, which says, "For He made Him [Jesus] who knew no sin to be sin [literally] for us, that [no matter what it looks or feels like], we might become the righteousness of God in Christ Jesus." You are abiding in His words, and His words are abiding in you. Thus, your desires are of your Father God, and He will cause you to always triumph over every temptation.

Jesus was tempted in all points yet without sin (Hebrews 4:15). He whipped temptation! You also have that power! You whipped temptation **in Jesus** some 2,000 years ago because He said you were crucified with Him. Glory! He took your sins and temptations with Him when He was nailed to the Cross. And because of what He did then, you are now the righteousness of God in Christ Jesus. So by all means apply this righteousness to every need, every care and every situation you face.

As we pray the Ephesians prayer, we must allow scriptures to speak to us, and then dare to worship the Lord with His Words by the power of the Spirit. If we do, the inward witness will grow stronger and stronger to us. By studying the Word of God and praying in this way, we become doers of the Word—not just hearers. No longer are we only casual readers observing the writings of a distant God. No longer do we study out of religious duty. Instead, we come to know Him. We come to know Him so well that the voice, the personality and the very Spirit of the Word become louder, more evident and an integral part of who we are and why we do what we do.

When we fellowship and commune with Him in this way, the great and mighty Spirit of God is given full expression to bear witness to things that are of Him in our lives. He's also able to bear witness and help us overcome things that are not of Him in our lives. Is that good news or what? Thank God it means we don't have to figure out everything in life for ourselves. The Spirit of God will bear witness to the plan of God for our lives.

He'll even get down to the nitty-gritty details and bear witness to the business idea He gave you. He will bear witness to people who are divine connections for you. He'll bear witness to the church you are to attend and bear witness to help you sidestep economic disaster. He will bear witness so you can walk in protection and escape harm. Friend, He will cause you to abide in Him and His words to abide in you. He will show you things to come. He will lead you, guide you, comfort you, help you and love you. Hallelujah!

It's so easy to follow Him, to know Him and to love Him. The plan and purpose of God is becoming clearer and clearer to you like a light from heaven so it's easy for you to obey Him and affect the lives of others. Hallelujah!

FINDING GOD'S WILL AT A CROSSROAD

After I had spent several years serving in various "helps" capacities in the local church, I found myself at a time of great transition in my life. I had always served gladly, volunteering in the local church and working a secular job. I had even traveled overseas to do some mission work and had recently returned to the states. But somehow my heart was hungering for something different.

The easy phrase of "something different" is not a lazy way to communicate this stirring. Actually, I describe it this way because if we are praying the Ephesians prayer, allowing the Word of God to provoke us and allowing the Holy Spirit free course to speak to us, then our hearts will stir when change is headed our way

You see, your heart or spirit is that part of you that contacts God. It's in your heart that you trust and believe in Him; it's not a head thing. So if you've been abiding in God's Word and His Word has been abiding in you, your heart will sense change when it comes. It will recognize that the promise you've been believing in is inching closer. Your heart, primed upon the Word of God, is able to see into the spirit realm by faith. So as you adopt a lifestyle that moves with God, your heart will begin to stir, quicken and provoke you when you approach a time of transition—a crossroads of decision or even an intersection of blessing.

Your head may be busy—your head or mind can be so very busy. Schedules and appointments demand your attention, and valid needs of daily existence need attention. You cannot stop living. Yet, at these times of subtle prompting, it's also important to set time apart to work with the Holy Spirit. It's important to respond to Him and sharpen your responses to the inward witness *for He is attempting to get you ready to meet your destiny.*

At these times of change, your heart may even begin to hunger and long for *something* you cannot pinpoint. Again, I vaguely say *something* because you may not know exactly what the *something* is that you're wanting. Yet, what you're probably sure of is that what you're currently doing or the place where you currently are doesn't "scratch" your "itch," so to speak.

It's like looking in the refrigerator over and over trying to find something to eat. Yet, even if your favorite foods stared you back in the face, you wouldn't be satisfied. The real truth is, you're not hungry for anything in front of you because you're hungry for *something different.* Ever been there? Jesus can help! He said, "I have meat to eat that you know not of, My meat is to do the will of Him Who sent me...." **So in times of transition and change, the first place God** *will draw you is to Himself.* Isn't that interesting? It's so right and true. Remember, we said in the beginning of the book: *You will find yourself in Him.*

I recall times in my own life when the Lord has drawn me. Actually, it reminds me of a tick in the woods. When we walk through the woods, somehow a tick can just land on us. We can more comically think of it this way. A tick is in the woods one day trekking around in his tennis shoes. He's got his worldly goods tied up in a bandanna on a stick, and the little guy is busy rehearsing in his heart, "I am off to see the world!" He watches and waits until a giant, vulnerable "sandaled" foot passes by.

Then like a vagabond intently watching train cars pass, he makes his move. He leaps on board and secures himself for the ride. For wherever the greater one ends up, so shall this little tick because where the greater one is, there shall he be also. That reminds me of an awesome scripture, and of course, the perfect example. John 14:3-4 says, "...Where I am, there you may be also. And where I go you know, and the way you know." Isn't that awesome! Wherever Jesus would have us to be within the harvest fields of the world, He will take us there. Glory! So in times of change, when the waters of our heart are restless and stirred, when there is a change stirring and an expectancy prompting us, we just leap onto the Lord Jesus. We must purpose to get closer to Him and secure ourselves at His feet. Then when He is ready to move in our lives; actually, we will simply move with Him into that blessing He has for us.

We must worship our Shepherd saying, "I am Your Sheep. I know Your voice. I am following You." Then as we worship *in the spirit and by the Spirit,* He shall gather us to Himself. He shall lead us into the green pasture that He has called us to labor in. He has a place of service for us—a place of green pasture where there's grass in the field for every man.

God's Word promises that blessed are those who hunger for those are the ones who get "filled with fulfillment." In my own life and example, I was hungry and thirsting and longing. So I took my hunger and my longing and dared to fan the flames of it. I did not ignore it, nor did I try to "feed it something else" to satisfy it. I did not read 20 Christian books. I did not buy a Christian figurine that said, "I love Jesus." I did not turn on a live worship CD and let someone else worship for me. I took truth and went to a small park in a nearby church after hours so workers did not think me deranged or insane. And there, in that private and serene place, I began to walk and to worship.

I want to be very clear here. Much is said of worship in Christian circles. Worship, worship, worship! But I'm not talking about singing or music. The type of worship that I'm speaking of can convert over into singing or be accompanied by music. Yet, I'm talking about taking a set of scriptures that have been highlighted to you and speaking them back to God in an attitude of thanksgiving. I'm talking about speaking these scriptures back to the Lord **as though these scriptures have already come to pass in your situation.** Dear one, I'm talking about rallying your understanding, focusing it, and making it praise God with these scriptures until joy and peace fill your heart.

Oh yes, that's what you need to do even if you feel like crying or feel like giving up or feel that things look *impossible*. Feelings are real, and there's no denying it. But faith is greater! God's Words are greater! So get by yourself and begin to speak these scriptures to the Lord with an attitude of "bless God, no matter what I feel like I will speak these scriptures as though they have already manifested." Speak them until joy and peace start to mount garrison over your mind and heart *because it is in this place that God will come to meet with you.*

John 4:23 boldly declares that God is *seeking* people who will worship Him **in this way.** Worshipping is not just about being able to sing a pretty song. The type of worship I speak of here is not based on singing at all. If it were, people who could not sing well would be disqualified. Some of us can only make a joyful noise. Yet, worshipping God by the inspiration of the Holy Spirit with the Word of Truth is what the Bible deems **true worship**. And worship is the highest form of prayer.

I did "sense" a little of what I was spiritually hungering for—for change and for my next place of ministry. But even with my "kind of knowing that," I did not start there. I did not start with my hunger, or with my perceptions, or with my thoughts or ideas. I started with the Word. I started by taking scriptures the Holy Spirit highlighted to me via the mighty Ephesians prayer and worshipped the Father. I started this way because I realized if the hunger, perceptions and promptings were from God, and I applied the "filter" or "author" of the Word then the promptings **of the Lord** would get even stronger.

I realized the "filter" of the Word and "author" of the Word would cause my perceptions to become progressively stronger until they overtook me and interrupted me. They would prove out as the passions and compassions of the Savior; His love and His desires would lead and compel me. I realized that His love and desires would cascade into the gifts of the Spirit, where the simple gift of prophecy, edification and comfort would come to me. I realized that He would empower me to prophesy to myself the very direction I needed. As His desires welled up in me then, whatever I asked, the answer would be yes and amen. So shall I bear fruit; so I shall glorify Him. And most blessed of all, so shall I become a consistent disciple.

When I went to the little park to talk to the Lord, I did not have a ministerial position or even open doors of ministerial opportunity. But, brother, when I hit joy in my heart as the realization of His leadings and His faithfulness to answer, I took it. I danced and shouted *before the seeming walls come down!* As I acknowledged that I heard His voice, that I followed that voice, and that I was led by Him, the walls of confusion also came down. That's your answer too! Don't wait to see whatever you're believing for in the natural realm. Worship until you run into peace and joy in the Holy Ghost, and then, dude, you're answer will so show up in the natural. Woo hoo!

A simple, faith-filled prayer had brought my answer. I began with the written Word of God. I knew I was called to the ministry so I began to worship the Lord with His words regarding ministry. I thanked Him for Ephesians 4:8, where it says that when Jesus ascended on high He gave gifts unto men. The Bible goes on to say that those "gifts" are apostles, prophets, evangelists, pastors and teachers for the work of the ministry to edify the saint.

I continued thanking God that I was called; I continued thanking Him that I was chosen. Then the

Holy Spirit began to flood scriptures up and out of my heart through my lips. I'd been abiding in Him by praying the Ephesians prayers and studying my Bible, and those "stockpiled" scriptures were abiding in me as I had been abiding in Him.

As always as I began to speak the Spirit supplied utterance. I thanked Him that I would be like Paul and "...finish my course with joy, and the ministry, which I have received of the Lord Jesus" (Acts 20:24 KJV). I thanked Him that by faith I am a finisher, and I would receive that crown that was laid up for me (2 Timothy 4:8). I thanked Him that He would grant unto me His servant that with all boldness I would speak forth His Word (Acts 4:29).

I thanked Him that He was opening unto me a door to speak the Word. I thanked Him that the Word of God would have free course through me and that the gifts and callings of God were "without repentance." Or in other words, God doesn't change His mind about those whom He calls. Then I boldly proclaimed with Paul in accordance with 1 Timothy 1:12, "Thank You, God, that You counted me faithful and are putting me into the ministry whereunto you have called me."

I also brought Acts 13:2 before Him. This is the verse where Paul was actually separated into his ultimate call. It's such a precious chapter because up until that time, Paul had already served as a preacher and a teacher for many years. Yet, the Bible tells us it was not until Acts 13 that he was separated into the actual work He was called to do. Acts 13:2 says, "...Separate me Barnabas and Saul for the work whereunto I have called them" (KJV). Who said so? Either a saint who was present moved by the gifts of the Spirit or an audible voice said so. But either way, the Holy Spirit said it was time to separate them unto Himself to begin their ultimate calling.

Paul was a walking, talking example of what we've discussed throughout this book. We've spoken of praying the Ephesians prayer and allowing scriptures to jump out at us. We've talked of going into the place of prayer and allowing that same inward witness of the Holy Spirit that leads us through the truth to then lead us in the place of prayer. And Paul so faithfully followed this pattern. Paul had so faithfully followed the Spirit of Truth, so faithfully followed the inward witness and so faithfully followed the enduement of the Trinity that now Acts 1:8 was taking place. The Holy Spirit had **made** Paul into a witness.

And now, the very One who had trained Paul, the same Spirit who led Paul, the same Spirit Paul had been faithful to—that Holy Spirit called Paul and ultimately separated Him. Essentially, the Spirit of God separated Paul even further unto Himself.

But please realize that you also can go further and deeper in God. If the Word leads you, you will go further into the Word. If the Spirit leads you, you will go further into the Spirit. If you allow Him to abide in You, You will find yourself abiding more and more and more in Him. When you follow the Lord, you will touch people's lives, and they will never be the same again. When you follow the Lord, it makes a pathway of truth and life able to lead you into a place He has prepared for you—a place in Him.

As I spoke these scriptures and the Holy Spirit astonished me with His agility and comprehensive technique, I simply began to speak what my heart wanted. I endeavored to utter in my understanding even some of the sharp and guttural longings within my heart. After all, the Word of God is the only tool sharp enough to dig that deep. The Word of God is the only tool able to discern what the mind-set of the Father is within the belly of your heart.

I did not see an angel; I did not pass out. Like you when you worship Him in this way, I hit a gusher of life and endeavored to wrap words around it. At that point of edification, excitement and joy, I simply began to utter what my heart truly desired. I spoke out things not necessarily specifically labeled in the Word of God, but nonetheless, were the Word of God to me. I began to speak the desires that had been born because the Word was abiding in me. I thanked the Lord that He had called me to teach about prayer and lead prayer. I thanked the Lord that He had called me to raise up groups of people to pray. I thanked Him that He had called me to help teach church members to pray for their pastors, to pray for the outpouring of the Holy Spirit, to pray for the government and to pray for laborers to reap the harvest. It was amazing!

The Holy Ghost had begun to bear witness to these phrases in the same way He would bear witness to scriptures in the Bible. Thus I knew these "things to come" that I had prayed out were as much the will of God as the books of the Bible written in black and white. I had tapped into the scroll written in heaven before I was ever born—the epistle of my life as it were. I had found my own "Book of Dana" in prayer, and there's a "Book of You" as well.

I thanked Him that He would use me to teach His dear saints how very easy it is to pray and that the saints *can* pray and do know His voice. I thanked Him that I would have a part in the prayer meetings of the last days that would serve as a catalyst for the very coming of the Lord. I thanked God that He would use my husband and me with regard to a move in "corporate" or *united prayer*. Hallelujah! It makes me shout even now. What I was saying was so inspired by the Holy Spirit that I began to laugh and shout. Honestly, I even felt a little tipsy—drunk (for lack of a better term) in the spirit. Woo hoo! A peace fell on me that seemed to pass up my understanding of how all this would come to pass. Actually, it was like I got so filled up with the Spirit that I was starting to understand the will of the Lord.

You may wonder: *Did anyone see you praying and acting like that in the little park?* Dude, at that point do you think I even cared? I mean, I wasn't being rude or obnoxious, and if someone had approached me I would most certainly have been kind and respectful. But so what if someone did see me acting all happy and joyous and shouting— maybe even a little "stoned" in the goodness of God. Most folks have seen so much of the contrary— Christians looking like they're constipated, worried, beaten down, frustrated, mad at the world and pickled instead of preserved. Don't you think it's about time the world sees some Acts 2 in Christians? "No, we are not drunk like what you suppose!" (Acts 2). We are, however, filled with *the* Spirit. Duuuuude— we are like sooo filled!

During that time of transition, I visited that little park often. Or I'd go to my apartment or sit in my car. I'd go wherever I needed to and however often

I needed to in order to get myself tanked up in peace and joy. I also continued going to the ministry where I volunteered and kept myself busy sowing time and prayer. I'd clean the ministry offices. The ministry had a huge beautiful prayer room with maps of the nations on the wall, and it was my favorite place to clean.

It wasn't long before the head of the ministry asked the Lord one day in prayer, "Lord, You told me You would give me a prayer coordinator. Where will I find this person to inspire prayer amongst the people, corral corporate prayer, pray for the ministry and raise up prayer groups?" The Lord answered him and said, "She's cleaning your prayer room."

I became the prayer coordinator for that ministry, and it was a position that had never existed before at that ministry. My job was to pray for the ministry and the leader who became the pastor. My job was also to teach about prayer, inspire the saints to pray and organize prayer groups. My job was to facilitate prayer individually in small groups and large gatherings so the plan of God could go forth in that ministry. I was praying with people "unitedly" all the time, and I ended up *doing the very things* I'd spoken out that day in prayer.

Wait! Were those things I'd spoken in prayer just my *desires*? Or had I been abiding in His Words and His Words had been truly abiding in *me* so much that His desires had literally become my desires? Had I prayed the Ephesians prayers so much that the Word became alive in me and chiseled out, sculpted and fashioned the very plans, purposes, pursuits, longings and abilities of God within me?

Truly, I could no longer tell where the Lord began and I ended. Looks like we became one! And isn't that how it should be?

I had abided in Him, and thus, He now truly abides—takes up residence, stretches out, lives, moves and has His being—in me. Therefore, the very things I desire, He desires; I but ask, and it actually gets done for me. Whatsoever things I desire are "His desires" so I ask them back to Him, for the desires came from Him. He asks through me, and so shall it be done. So shall I bear fruit. So shall I glorify Him—and most blessed of all—so shall I be His disciple.

I believe the Lord literally created that prayer coordinator position for me at the ministry where I volunteered. It was my first major step into the ministry, and I entered through the doorway of my very own mouth. Those times of prayer and worship with the Lord trained me and still today I'm walking out what was prayed in those days at the park.

Of course, I still spend time praying and worshipping my Savior on the heels of Bible study via the Ephesians prayer. I pray the Ephesians prayer every time I get ready to study my Bible or every time I get ready to pray. Times of prayer are eternal.

Today I'm walking out the fruit of my prayers that began at the park. I teach on prayer everywhere I go and help raise up prayer for ministries. I get to help the individual Christian—no matter how old, how young, how newly saved or how anciently saved—realize how very easy it is to pray. It's my privilege to see folks break open under the power of the Holy Spirit and recognize the new creation they really are in Christ Jesus. I get to experience the delight of my Savior as He manifests Himself through those He loves so dearly, those that He calls His very body. I have the blessed responsibility of watching the same Holy Spirit become diverse and multifaceted as He expresses Himself through *each and every believer.*

Oh, dear one. You are greatly loved and Jesus paid a great price for *you.* He paid a price for your healing. He paid a price *so great* that you can only depend upon revelation to bring understanding to you. He paid a price for your peace, your children, your direction and your prosperity. He paid a price spirit, soul and body in order for you to miss hell and gain heaven.

However, dear one, please remember that Jesus also paid a heavy price so you could have **fellowship with Him**. He suffered separation from the Father so you could be close to Him—so close that you're literally **in Him.**

Never forget that you **are in Him**, dear one. You know Him, you know His voice, and you are following Him. At the very moment you received Jesus as your Lord, you were no longer bound for hell. At that moment, the blessing of going to heaven when you die became yours! And in that moment, dear one, you also came to know *Him.* Oh, yes, it's true.

If you could hear His voice to get saved *even as a rank sinner* and followed Him into the new birth, **then you most certainly know Him and can follow Him now—TODAY!** You do hear His voice. You are His sheep. You have the mind of Christ, and you have an anointing from the Holy One. Even as a babe in the Lord, out of your mouth comes perfected praise. The blood of Jesus says so for it speaks better things.

My dearest brother and sister, *don't ever doubt it, but determine to always decree it, shout it, rejoice in it and dance about it because...*

YOU CAN PRAY!

CHAPTER **17**

THE MOST IMPORTANT PRAYER OF ALL—**DOWNLOADING** YOUR **SPIRITUAL SOFTWARE**

One prayer stands above all the rest—it's the most important prayer of all.

Of course, the emphasis of this book is the great and powerful prayer found in Ephesians 1:17-23 and how the Holy Ghost will lead you through the Word, in prayer and in every aspect of your life. There are also many other powerful epistle prayers. Just to name a few, there are prayers found in Ephesians 3:14-21, Philippians 1:9, Colossians 1:9 and 3 John 2. There is a "model" of prayer in Matthew 6:9, not to mention the many scriptures that can be prayed or spoken on a daily basis. You can worship God in the spirit with a truth. There are so many prayers and so many ways to pray God's Word.

However, one prayer alone is the most important prayer of all. In comparison, the great and mighty Ephesians prayer and every other prayer in the epistles are but a *volume control*. As a Christian prays these prayers, the volume of the voice and leading of the Holy Spirit is turned up "louder." These prayers are better than any hi-tech tuning apparatus.

For instance, when you drive from one city to another or one district to another, you may need to *fine-tune* your radio dial to bring in better reception as your location changes. So it is with the epistle prayers, which cause the voice and inward witness of the Holy Spirit to be "louder" and fine-tune your heart so His powerful leadings, promptings and confirmations come in clearer.

These prayers are vital!

Still, the volume and fine-tuning knobs are of *no use* if you don't have a sound system installed.

Think about it for a minute.

If you don't have a satellite radio, it doesn't matter how powerful your car radio is. You have to have the satellite radio unit installed before you can get signals. It's the same with a car radio. If the radio in your car isn't hooked up, volume and clarity of reception are totally irrelevant. That makes sense, doesn't it? Bottom line, you must have the equipment and the hardware installed before you can mess with reception.

The same is true with *you!* We've talked a lot about prayers that will help you get better reception and turn up the volume. But we also need to make sure you have the right hardware installed. The sound system you are looking for is the Holy Spirit coming to live and make residence in your heart. The Holy Spirit, the third person of the Godhead, will come to reside in your heart the minute you receive Jesus Christ as your Lord and Savior.

Beep. Beep. Beep. Beep. We interrupt this scheduled programming with a news bulletin alert: **Jesus Christ is alive and well and broadcasting 24 hours a day!** He's broadcasting the news, *The Good News.* He's broadcasting that Jesus Christ paid the price for your salvation and healing by His work on the Cross.

News flash: You are not going to die; you are going to live and declare the works of the Lord. We take you now to the "Will-of-God-Cam." What do you know, there's the Lord Jesus Christ right now in the field showing you the group of people whose lives you are called to affect. We cut back to the studio, and Jesus is showing you a plan to revive that ailing business. Even the weather report on the news is good. Your skies may have been blue, but they're sunny now! Dark clouds are scattering; the Light has come.

This just in. Well, actually, it came in more than 2,000 years ago. You can know that you will go to heaven when you die. You can ask Jesus into your heart right now and instantly experience the peace of mind that only Jesus can give. Experience that "sudden deep peace"—peace that goes beyond your questions, peace that settles in upon you even before you see the answers to your problems. For you see, it's clear and simple:

JESUS IS THE ANSWER!

Hook up with Him, and He will take care of everything else. Pray this simple prayer with me right now—wherever you are. If you are in a hotel room, bow down by the bed. If you're in a car or in an airplane seat, just bow your heart.

God will look upon the heart as you pray this

prayer. It's not a rigid, must-pray-verbatim prayer. It's simply a prototype, a format, a shoe horn to help you install a sound system in your heart.

Before you begin praying, read this scripture aloud to yourself. It will crystallize things for you!

Romans 10:9 says, "If you confess with your mouth the Lord Jesus and believe in your heart that God has raised Him from the dead, you will be saved. "

Now, dear one, let's pray this prayer together. It will help you!

Father God, I believe Jesus died and rose again for me. Jesus, I ask You to come into my heart. Jesus, thank You for loving me. Thank You for coming into my heart. Thank you that I will never be alone again. Thank You that I am now a Christian. Thank You that my sound system is installed. Thank You that I can hear Your voice and follow Your leadings. Thank You that when I do die someday, I will go to heaven. And thank You that I will never be the same again.

Hallelujah! There is the peace, the joy, the change right there. You'll never, ever be the same again. There *is* the sound system. God loves you no matter what you've ever done before. If you prayed this prayer and meant it with all your heart, no matter what sin you have ever committed—you are forgiven. It's that simple, and you have God's Word on it. The Bible says, "...Thou shalt call his name JESUS: for he shall save his people from their sins" (Matthew 1:21 KJV). You are forgiven of the sins of the past, and He will help you with your future.

Dear New One: Please see the final pages of this

book for phone numbers and addresses. You can call, e-mail or write us, and we will send you literature to help you go further in Jesus Christ. We can also help you find a church. Pray and ask God to help you find a good church and give you wonderful Christian friends to help you walk along the way. He will give you the most wonderful comrades and people for your life.

Then, dear new one, do what you've learned in this book. Pray the prayer found in Ephesians 1:17-23, and read your Bible in the New Testament so scriptures can jump out at you. Write down those scriptures and what you feel the Lord is saying to you about them. Then go into prayer and pray the Ephesians prayer. Pray as far in your understanding as you can. Then pray the Ephesians prayer over yourself regarding your job and your relationships, even regarding finding a church. The Lord will give you wisdom and revelation regarding your employment, your friends, your boss and ultimately your purpose and calling in life.

How exciting for you! Hallelujah! You are now a child of the King! God bless you, dear one.

~Dana~

COMING SOON!

You Can Pray - Part 2:
The Exceeding Greatness of His Power

by Dana Shrader

To order additional copies of
***You Can Pray,* contact:**

youcanpray.net

Lonnie & Dana

shrader ministries

For a complete listing of teaching
materials or more information
about their ministry,
contact:

**DANA SHRADER
P.O. BOX 2367
SANTA BARBARA, CA 93120**

myprayerschool.com
info@youcanpray.net
918-845-0811

CPSIA information can be obtained at www.ICGtesting.com
Printed in the USA
LVOW010554091111

254167LV00004B/4/P